THE MEETING HOUSE

2 Litchfield Road
Londonderry, NH 03053
Meetinghouseofnhdems@gmail.com

Rebooting the American Dream

Also by Thom Hartmann

*Unequal Protection: How Corporations Became "People"
—and How You Can Fight Back*

Threshold: The Crisis of Western Culture

*Cracking the Code: How to Win Hearts, Change
Minds, and Restore America's Original Vision*

*Screwed: The Undeclared War against the Middle
Class—and What We Can Do about It*

What Would Jefferson Do?: A Return to Democracy

*The Last Hours of Ancient Sunlight: The Fate of the
World and What We Can Do Before It's Too Late*

*Ultimate Sacrifice: John and Robert Kennedy, the Plan
for a Coup in Cuba, and the Murder of JFK*

Legacy of Secrecy: The Long Shadow of the JFK Assassination

We the People: A Call to Take Back America

*Walking Your Blues Away: How to Heal the Mind
and Create Emotional Well-being*

Attention Deficit Disorder : A Different Perception

*Thom Hartmann's Complete Guide to ADHD: Help
for Your Family at Home, School and Work*

*Healing ADD : Simple Exercises That
Will Change Your Daily Life*

The Edison Gene: ADHD and the Gift of the Hunter Child

*ADD Success Stories: A Guide to Fulfillment for
Families with Attention Deficit Disorder*

Think Fast: The ADD Experience

Beyond ADD: Hunting for Reasons in the Past and Present

*ADHD Secrets of Success: Coaching Yourself to
Fulfillment in the Business World*

The Prophet's Way: A Guide to Living in the Now

The Greatest Spiritual Secret of the Century

Rebooting the American Dream

11 Ways to Rebuild Our Country

Thom Hartmann

BK

Berrett–Koehler Publishers, Inc.
San Francisco
a BK Currents book

Berrett-Koehler Publishers, Inc.

235 Montgomery Street, Suite 650, San Francisco, CA 94104-2916

Tel: (415) 288-0260   Fax: (415) 362-2512   www.bkconnection.com

Ordering Information

Quantity sales. Special discounts are available on quantity purchases by corporations, associations, and others. For details, contact the "Special Sales Department" at the Berrett-Koehler address above.

Individual sales. Berrett-Koehler publications are available through most bookstores. They can also be ordered directly from Berrett-Koehler:

Tel: (800) 929-2929; Fax: (802) 864-7626; www.bkconnection.com.

Orders for college textbook/course adoption use. Please contact Berrett-Koehler:

Tel: (800) 929-2929; Fax: (802) 864-7626.

Orders by U.S. trade bookstores and wholesalers. Please contact Ingram Publisher Services, Tel: (800) 509-4887; Fax: (800) 838-1149; E-mail: customer.service@ ingrampublisherservices.com; or visit www.ingrampublisherservices.com/Ordering for details about electronic ordering.

Berrett-Koehler and the BK logo are registered trademarks of Berrett-Koehler Publishers, Inc.

Printed in the United States of America

Berrett-Koehler books are printed on long-lasting acid-free paper. When it is available, we choose paper that has been manufactured by environmentally responsible processes. These may include using trees grown in sustainable forests, incorporating recycled paper, minimizing chlorine in bleaching, or recycling the energy produced at the paper mill.

Library of Congress Cataloging-in-Publication Data
Hartmann, Thom, 1951–
    Rebooting the American dream : 11 ways to rebuild our country / Thom Hartmann.
      p. cm.
    Includes bibliographical references and index.
    ISBN 978-1-60509-706-0 (pbk. : alk. paper)
  1. Political planning—United States. 2. United States—Economic policy—2009–
I. Title. II. Title: Eleven ways to rebuild our country.
    JK468.P64H37 2010
    330.973—dc22

                                            2010023170

15 14 13 12 11 10   10 9 8 7 6 5 4 3 2 1

Cover/jacket Designer: Ian Shimkoviak/ The Book Designers
Interior design and composition by Gary Palmatier, Ideas to Images
Elizabeth von Radics, copyeditor; Mike Mollett, proofreader; Medea Minnich, indexer.

DEDICATION

To our daughters, Kindra and Kerith,
who are coincidentally both back in school
and rebooting their own lives.

May the world you inherit be as rich in wonder and
opportunity as the world into which your parents were born.

Thank you both for being such wonderful, caring,
and honorable human beings, so dedicated to
healing the world one person at a time.

Contents

Introduction: Back to the Future   1

CHAPTER 1   Bring My Job Home!   17

CHAPTER 2   Roll Back the Reagan Tax Cuts   33

CHAPTER 3   Stop Them from Eating My Town   51

CHAPTER 4   An Informed and Educated Electorate   65

CHAPTER 5   Medicare "Part E"—for Everybody   81

CHAPTER 6   Make Members of Congress
Wear NASCAR Patches   97

CHAPTER 7   Cool Our Fever   123

CHAPTER 8   They Will Steal It!   139

CHAPTER 9   Put Lou Dobbs out to Pasture   153

CHAPTER 10   Wal-Mart Is *Not* a Person   169

CHAPTER 11   In the Shadow of the Dragon   191

Conclusion: Tag, You're It!   199

Acknowledgments   203

Notes   205

Index   217

About the Author   229

Introduction:
Back to the Future

I know no safe depository of the ultimate powers of the society but the people themselves; and if we think them not enlightened enough to exercise their control with a wholesome discretion, the remedy is not to take it from them, but to inform their discretion by education. This is the true corrective of abuses of constitutional power.

—Thomas Jefferson, letter to William
Charles Jarvis, September 28, 1820

ON APRIL 14, 1789, GEORGE WASHINGTON WAS OUT WALKING through the fields at Mount Vernon, his home in Virginia, when Charles Thomson, the secretary of the Continental Congress, rode up on horseback. Thomson had a letter for Washington from the president pro tempore of the new, constitutionally created United States Senate, telling Washington that he'd just been elected president and the inauguration was set for April 30 in the nation's capital, New York City.[1]

This created two problems for Washington.

The first was saying goodbye to his 82-year-old mother, which the 57-year-old Washington did that night. She gave him her blessing and told him it was the last time he'd see her alive, as she was gravely ill; and, indeed, she died before he returned from New York.

The second problem was finding a suit of clothes made in America. For that he sent a courier to his old friend and fellow general from the American Revolutionary War, Henry Knox.

Washington couldn't find a suit made in America because in the years prior to the American Revolution, the British East India Company (whose tea was thrown into Boston Harbor by outraged colonists after the Tea Act of 1773 gave the world's largest transnational corporation a giant tax break) controlled the manufacture and the transportation of a whole range of goods, including fine clothing. Cotton and wool could be grown and sheared in the colonies, but it had to be sent to England to be turned into clothes.

This was a routine policy for England, and it is why until India achieved its independence in 1947 Mahatma Gandhi (who was assassinated a year later) sat with his spinning wheel for his lectures and spun daily in his own home. It was, like his Salt March, a protest against the colonial practices of England and an entreaty to his fellow Indians to make their own clothes to gain independence from British companies and institutions.

Fortunately for George Washington, an American clothing company had been established on April 28, 1783, in Hartford, Connecticut, by a man named Daniel Hinsdale, and it produced high-quality woolen and cotton clothing as well as items made from imported silk.[2] It was to Hinsdale's company that Knox turned, and he helped Washington get—in time for his inauguration two weeks later—a nice, but not excessively elegant, brown American-made suit. (He wore British black later for the celebrations and the most famous painting.)

When Washington became president in 1789, most of America's personal and industrial products of any significance were manufactured in England or in its colonies. Washington asked his Treasury secretary, Alexander Hamilton, what could be done about that, and Hamilton came up with an 11-point plan to foster American manufacturing, which he presented to Congress in 1791. By 1793 most of its points had either been made into law by Congress or formulated into policy by either President Washington or the various states, which put the country on a path of developing its industrial base and generating the largest source of federal revenue for more than a hundred years.

Those strategic proposals built the greatest industrial powerhouse the world had ever seen and, after more than 200 successful years, were abandoned only during the administrations of Ronald Reagan, George H. W. Bush, and Bill Clinton (and remain abandoned to this day). Modern-day China, however, implemented most of Hamilton's plan and has brought about a remarkable transformation of its nation in a single generation.

Hamilton's 11-point plan for "American manufactures" is a primary inspiration for this book (see sidebar). It was part of a larger work titled *Alexander Hamilton's Report on the Subject of Manufactures: Made in His Capacity of Secretary of the Treasury.*

Alexander Hamilton's 11-point Plan for "American Manufactures"

A full view having now been taken of the inducements to the promotion of manufactures in the United States, accompanied with an examination of the principal objections which are commonly urged in *opposition,* it is proper, in the next place, to consider the means by which it may be effected....

In order to a better judgment of the means proper to be resorted to by the United States, it will be of use to advert to those which have been employed with success in other countries. The principal of these are—

I. Protecting duties [import taxes, now called "tariffs"]— or duties on those foreign articles which are the rivals of the domestic ones intended to be encouraged.

Duties of this nature evidently amount to a virtual bounty on the domestic fabrics, since by enhancing the charges on foreign articles, they enable the national manufacturers to undersell all their foreign competitors.…[I]t has the additional recommendation of being a resource of revenue. Indeed, all the duties imposed on imported articles, though with an exclusive view to revenue, have the effect in contemplation; and, except where they fill on raw materials, wear a beneficent aspect towards the manufacturers of the country.

II. Prohibitions of rival articles, or duties equivalent to prohibitions.

This is another and an efficacious mean of encouraging national manufactures;…Of duties equivalent to prohibitions, there are examples in the laws of the United States…but they are not numerous.…*[I]t might almost be said, by the principles of distributive justice; certainly by the duty of endeavoring to secure to their own citizens a reciprocity of advantages.*

III. Prohibitions of the exportation of the materials of manufactures.

The desire of securing a cheap and plentiful supply for the national workmen, and, where the article is either peculiar to the country, or of peculiar quality there, the jealousy of enabling foreign workmen to rival those of the nation with its own materials, are the leading motives to this species of regulation.…It is seen at once, that its immediate operation is to abridge the demand and keep down the price of the produce of some other branch of industry, generally speaking, of agriculture, to the prejudice of those who carry it on; and though if it be really essential to the prosperity of any very important national manufacture, it may happen that those who are injured in the first instance, may be eventually indemnified, by the superior steadiness of an extensive domestic market depending on that prosperity: yet in a matter, in which there is so much room for nice and difficult combinations, in which such opposite considerations combat each other, prudence seems to dictate, that the expedient in question ought to be indulged with a sparing hand.

IV. Pecuniary bounties.

This has been found one of the most efficacious means of encouraging manufactures, and it is in some views the best; though it has not yet been practised upon by the government of the United States, (unless the allowance on the exportion of dried and pickled fish and salted meat, could be considered as a bounty,) and though it is less favoured by public opinion than some other modes, its advantages are these—

1. It is a species of encouragement more positive and direct than any other, and for that very reason, has a more immediate tendency to stimulate and uphold new enterprises, increasing the chances of profit, and diminishing the risks of loss, in the first attempts.

2. It avoids the inconvenience of a temporary augmentation of price, which is incident to some other modes, or it produces it to a less degree; either by making no addition to the charges on the rival foreign article, as in the case of protecting duties, or by making a smaller addition. The first happens when the fund for the bounty is derived from a different object (which may or may not increase the price of some other article, according to the nature of that object); the second when the fund is derived from the same or a similar object of foreign manufacture. One per cent duty on the foreign article converted into a bounty on the domestic, will have an equal effect with a duty of two per cent exclusive of such bounty; and the price of the foreign commodity is liable to be raised, in the one case, in the proportion of one per cent; in the other, in that of two per cent. Indeed, the bounty, when drawn from another source, is calculated to promote a reduction of price; because, without laying any new charge on the foreign

article, it serves to introduce a competition with it, and to increase the total quantity of the article in the market.

3. Bounties have not, like high protecting duties, a tendency to produce scarcity....

4. Bounties are sometimes not only the best, but the only proper expedient, for uniting the encouragement of a new object....

The true way to conciliate these two interests, is to lay a duty on foreign manufactures, of the material, the growth of which is desired to be encouraged, and to apply the produce of that duty by way of bounty, either upon the production of the material itself, or upon its manufacture at home, or upon both....

[P]ecuniary bounties are in most cases indispensable to the intro-duction of a new branch....Bounties are especially essential, in regard to articles, upon which those foreigners who have been ac-customed to supply a country, are in the practice of granting them.

The continuance of bounties on manufactures long established, must almost always be of questionable policy; because a pre-sumption would arise in every such case, that there were natural and inherent impediments to success But in new undertakings, they are as justifiable, as they are oftentimes necessary....

V. Premiums.

These are of a nature allied to bounties, though distinguishable from them in some important features.

Bounties are applicable to the whole quantity of an article produced or manufactured, or exported, and involve a corre-spondent expense—Premiums serve to reward some particular excellence or superiority, some extraordinary exertion or skill, and are dispensed only in a small number of cases. But their ef-fect is to stimulate general effort....

VI. The exemption of the [raw] materials of manufactures from duty.

The policy of that exemption, as a general rule, particularly in reference to new establishments, is obvious....Of a nature, bearing some affinity to that policy, is the regulation which exempts from duty the tools and implements, as well as the books, clothes, and household furniture of foreign artists, who come to reside in the United States; an advantage already secured to them by the laws of the Union, and which it is, in every view, proper to continue.

VII. Drawbacks of the duties which are imposed on the materials of manufactures....

[S]uch drawbacks are familiar in countries which systematically pursue the business of manufactures; which furnishes an argument for the observance of a similar policy in the United States; and the idea has been adopted by the laws of the Union, in the instances of salt and molasses. It is believed that it will be found advantageous to extend it to some other articles.

VIII. The encouragement of new inventions and discoveries, at home, and of the introduction into the United States of such as may have been made in other countries; particularly, those which relate to machinery.

This is among the most useful and unexceptionable of the aids which can be given to manufactures. The usual means of that encouragement are pecuniary rewards, and, for a time, exclusive privileges. The first must be employed, according to the occasion, and the utility of the invention, or discovery. For the last, so far as respects "authors and inventors," provision has been made by law....

It is customary with manufacturing nations to prohibit, under severe penalties, the exportation of implements and machines, which they have either invented or improved....As far as prohibitions tend to prevent foreign competitors from deriving the benefit of the improvements made at home, they tend to increase the advantages of those by whom they may have been introduced; and operate as an encouragement to exertion.

IX. Judicious regulations for the inspection of manufactured commodities.

This is not among the least important of the means by which the prosperity of manufactures may be promoted. It is, indeed, in many cases one of the most essential. Contributing to prevent frauds upon consumers at home, and exporters to foreign countries—to improve the quality and preserve the character of the national manufactures…

X. The facilitating of pecuniary remittances from place to place—

Is a point of considerable moment to trade in general, and to manufactures in particular; by rendering more easy the purchase of raw materials and provisions, and the payment for manufactured supplies. A general circulation of bank paper, which is to be expected from the institution lately established, will be a most valuable mean to this end.

XI. The facilitating of the transportation of commodities.

Improvements favouring this object intimately concern all the domestic interests of a community; but they may without impropriety be mentioned as having an important relation to manufactures. There is perhaps scarcely any thing, which has been better calculated to assist the manufacturers of Great Britain, than the meliorations of the public roads of that kingdom, and the great progress which has been of late made in opening canals. Of the former, the United States stand much in need…

These examples, it is to be hoped, will stimulate the exertions of the government and citizens of every state. There can certainly be no object, more worthy of the cares of the local administrations; and it were to be wished, that there was no doubt of the power of the national government to lend its direct aid, on a comprehensive plan. This is one of those improvements, which could be prosecuted with more efficacy by the whole, than by any part or parts of the Union.…

The following remarks are sufficiently judicious and pertinent to deserve a literal quotation: "Good roads, canals, and navigable rivers, by diminishing the expense of carriage, put the remote parts of a country more nearly upon a level with those in the neighborhood of a town. They are upon that account, the greatest of all improvements."…

It may confidently be affirmed, that there is scarcely any thing, which has been devised, better calculated to excite a general spirit of improvement, than the institutions of this nature. They are truly invaluable.

In countries where there is great private wealth, much may be effected by the voluntary contributions of patriotic individuals; but *in a community situated like that of the United States, the public purse must supply the deficiency of private resource. In what can it be so useful as in prompting and improving the efforts of industry?*

All which is humbly submitted.

Alexander Hamilton
Secretary of the Treasury

Note: This excerpt has been edited for length by the author, eliminating Hamilton's debate with Jefferson over an industry- versus agriculture-based economy. The italics are Hamilton's.

Source: http://www.archive.org/details/alexanderhamilt00caregoog

Hamilton looked at the nation and determined what needed to be done to rebuild the country after the Revolutionary War had devastated it and subservience to England's Tudor Plan "free trade" policies had left Americans without any significant domestic industrial base.

In the same tradition, this book goes through 11 steps we can take today to rebuild our country in the wake of the devastation of 30 years of Reaganomics and how we can recover the industrial base we've lost to the "free trade/flat earth" idiocy of the Reagan-Bush-Clinton-Bush era.

11 Ways

Chapter 1, "Bring My Job Home!" covers how economies work and why we need to heed Alexander Hamilton's advice. It points out that simply moving money around or creating a service economy ("Do you want fries with that?") doesn't produce long-lasting wealth in a country; only manufacturing does. Political economist Adam Smith pointed out that it's the application of human labor to raw materials—his example was turning a tree branch into an axe handle—that fuels a growing economy. We've gone from more than 20 percent of our economy being based on manufacturing before Reagan to around 11 percent now. This has left us in the precarious position of being unable to make a missile or an aircraft carrier that we may need if we have to defend Taiwan from China without parts from the communist dictatorship of China. These "free trade/flat earth" policies are stupid on national security grounds as much as anything else, but their major impact has been to dismantle the American middle class and consequently put our democracy itself at risk.

Chapter 2, "Roll Back the Reagan Tax Cuts," points out how when top income-tax rates on millionaires and billionaires are above 50 percent, not only does the gap between the very rich and the working poor shrink but the nation's economy stabilizes and grows. One of the most interesting features of this chapter is a little-known study done by the chairman of the libertarian Cato Institute, which found that Ronald Reagan's and George W. Bush's tax cuts actually *stimulated the growth* of the size of government, whereas the higher taxes that had preceded Reagan and the increased taxes under Clinton (passed into law without a single Republican vote) actually *shrank* the size of government.

Chapter 3, "Stop Them from Eating My Town," covers the ground of monopoly- and crony-capitalism, an economic system born and bred when Reagan stopped enforcing the Sherman Antitrust Act of 1890. From too-big-to-fail to too-big-to-allow-competition, oligarchic corporations have come to dominate virtually every major sector of the American economy; the result has been the devastation of local economies and the prevention of new entrepreneurial small ventures. In the 200 years before Reagan, the downtowns and the business districts of every city in this nation were unique—and locally owned and operated. There was a certain inefficiency associated with it, but that inefficiency guaranteed healthy local businesses and communities. Only when we roll back Reagan's hands-off policies on Big Business and re-embrace the "trust-busting" practices of Republican Theodore Roosevelt will we see a revitalization of Main Streets across America.

Chapter 4, "An Informed and Educated Electorate," begins by showing how badly our news media has deteriorated, how it caters only to what people want and not to what they need, and how important it is that we take our media back from the profit-hungry monopolies that have abandoned the public-service mission of media. This chapter also tells the story of Thomas Jefferson's dream—made explicit when he founded the University of Virginia as this nation's first *free* college—that every American, regardless of birth or station, should be able to get an education from primary school through postgraduate university programs—*at no cost.* Spending on the education of young people pays back handsomely when they go on to make the society richer and, because of their higher incomes, provide higher income-tax revenues. When Reagan took a budgetary axe to the University of California and ended its free admissions policy, he handed to the countries of Europe and Asia the opportunity to overtake us in everything from patent applications to doctor-to-patient ratios to excellence in engineering and invention. And they've taken that opportunity. We need to take it back.

Chapter 5, "Medicare 'Part E'—for Everybody," points out how a nation that liberates its citizens from worrying about getting proper medical care is a nation of entrepreneurs, innovators, and stress-free families. It's also a nation that can successfully compete internationally for manufacturing work, when companies are free of health insurance burdens. Instead of handing off trillions of dollars to for-profit health insurance companies—which are forbidden by law in *every other industrialized nation on earth* from providing basic health insurance—we have attached giant corporate leeches to our own backs. The salt we need to pour on them is a national single-payer health insurance system—simply by expanding Medicare to include all Americans and plugging the loopholes in it that have been drilled by corporate lobbyists and their wholly-owned prostitutes...er...politicians.

Chapter 6, "Make Members of Congress Wear NASCAR Patches," tackles the problem of our private money–fueled electoral system and all the havoc it has wreaked. We need to fix—seal, really—the revolving door between government and industry; repair our monetary, investment, and banking systems; and change how we finance campaigns in this country. The idea of public financing of campaigns has recently been made very problematic by five Republicans on the U.S. Supreme Court, who ruled in 2010 that corporations are "persons" with full "free speech" rights under the First Amendment. This chapter offers some workarounds, and chapter 10 takes on the problem of the Court's decision directly.

Chapter 7, "Cool Our Fever," shows the incredible problems that arise from our own addiction to oil, especially in transportation, and it calls out the corporations and the billionaires who are making fortunes by pumping carbon into our atmosphere, putting all life on earth at risk—including us. The solutions include a carbon tax, but we must act soon.

Chapter 8, "They Will Steal It!" is based on one of the greatest foreign policy insights I've ever gotten, shared with me by activist and comedian Dick Gregory at around 3:00 A.M. as we were well into our third glass of wine and about five miles above the Atlantic Ocean on our way to Uganda. It is about how we cannot force other countries through military might to adopt our values of democracy and an open society—and how they will steal our ideas and our values if we engage them constructively so they can see how they can benefit from those ideals. It's high time that America became less dependent on the military by cutting back the Pentagon, by bringing back the draft, and by returning to a functional democratic republic like our Founders envisioned and most of the developed countries of the world enjoy.

Chapter 9, "Put Lou Dobbs out to Pasture," addresses the problem of what's popularly referred to as "illegal immigration," when, in reality, it is a problem of economics and illegal hiring by American companies. The problem started in 1986, when Reagan granted a blanket amnesty to millions of people who'd come into this country illegally, declared war on unions, and thus broke down the main barrier to entry to the workforce for people here without citizenship. The result has been more than 10 million noncitizens flowing across our borders (from countries all over the world—many come in on tourist or student visas and simply stay after their visa has expired), producing a massive dilution of the labor market. Add to that incendiary mixture a few right-wing racists pointing out the immigrants and telling frightened American workers, "Those *brown people* want your jobs!" and you have an explosive brew. We can fix all of this by cracking down on companies illegally hiring "undocumented workers" and by tightening the labor market to shore up wages for American workers.

Chapter 10, "Wal-Mart Is *Not* a Person," tells the story of how back in the 1880s corporations—then the railroad corporations, the giants of the Robber Baron Era—turned to the U.S. Supreme Court to give them human rights under the Constitution. Although the Court didn't actually do that, the court reporter *wrote* that they did, and for 130 years we've seen the creeping encroachment of the corporate form into rights our Founders fought and died for to give exclusively to humans. The pinnacle of this came in 2010 when the Supreme Court ruled that corporations are people and have political free-speech rights to spend millions, even billions, of dollars for or against political candidates and ballot initiatives. The result—if not fixed soon—will be the complete transformation of this country from a democracy into a corporate plutocracy. We need to block the Court in this superactivist behavior by amending the Constitution to say that only *humans* are "people."

Chapter 11, "In the Shadow of the Dragon," tells the story of a visit to the Mondragon Cooperative headquarters in the town of the same name in the Basque region of Spain in late 2009. We saw one of the world's largest *worker-owned* businesses, with more than 90,000 employees turning over more than $14 billion a year worldwide. There are alternatives to the traditional top-down investor-owned corporate form, and people around the world are increasingly embracing these alternatives because they are better for local communities, better for the workforce, and better for the environment. The only losers are billionaires, particularly those who own most of our media and thus never tell you that every corporation in Germany, for example, must have at least 50 percent of its board of directors coming directly from the ranks of labor.

The conclusion, "Tag, You're It!" is about tried-and-true methods—most that we've used before in this country and all that we've at least flirted with—that can bring back a strong middle class and restore America to stability and prosperity without endangering future generations. It's straightforward, easily understood, and the only obstacle to implementing virtually every chapter's suggestion is the power of vast wealth (usually corporate wealth). Past presidents—most famously Teddy and Franklin Roosevelt—have openly challenged that corporate power, and the time has come for the current or next president (and Congress) to do the same. But they won't if *We the People* don't demand it.

This book is an outline to lay down those demands. Good luck!

CHAPTER **1**

Bring My Job Home!

> *By preferring the support of domestic to that of foreign industry,* he [the entrepreneur] intends only his own security, and by directing that industry in such a manner as its produce may be of the greatest value, he intends only his own gain, and he is in this, as in many other cases, led by an invisible hand to promote an end which was no part of his intention.
>
> —Adam Smith, *Wealth of Nations,* 1776*

THE WHITE HOUSE CALLED ME.

About a year after President Barack Obama took office, on the first anniversary of his major economic recovery legislation, his administration was struggling to get the word out that the legislation was, in fact, quite a success story. I found myself invited to the White House as part of a small group of well-known authors and bloggers to meet with a top administration economist as part of this promotion effort.

It was an odd problem they were facing, given that this president was masterful during the 2008 election campaign in communicating his ideas and his vision to the American public. So what happened? Why didn't America know that the $787 billion legislation represented one of the largest middle-class tax cuts in American history, that it had demonstrably created or preserved

---

*Emphasis added to rebut "free trade" misuse of this quote, as free-traders always drop the first 11 words.

between 1.5 million and 3 million jobs, and that it had, in all probability, prevented the severe recession Obama inherited from George W. Bush from turning into a second Republican Great Depression, at least in the short term?

Part of the problem was that the Democrats hadn't much mentioned or marketed the legislation leading up to the one-year anniversary, nor had they given it a catchy name—a "New Deal" or "Contract with America" sort of thing—leaving it instead as a "stimulus bill" (officially called the American Recovery and Reinvestment Act of 2009).

A second problem was that a lot of the Republicans in Congress—the Disloyal Opposition—were blatantly lying to the American public about the bill's impact, saying it had created absolutely no jobs. Adding insult to injury, they were simultaneously attending ribbon-cutting and check-giving ceremonies in their own districts, celebrating its successes—even though they all voted against it. Most of the corporate media didn't bother to even mention the irony or hypocrisy of this.

The Democrats in Congress and the Obama administration had, in fact, crafted and passed legislation that moved money into the hands and the pockets of working people, who spent virtually all of it, which fueled the economy by direct stimulation and its multiplier effect, as intended. The bill reduced both tax and deduction rates for working people and poured billions of dollars into programs designed to get people to buy new products—programs like the $3 billion "Cash for Clunkers," which offered incentives for people to trade in gas guzzlers for fuel-efficient vehicles.

What drove the legislation was precisely what drove Franklin D. Roosevelt's New Deal, which got us out of the Great Depression: Keynesian economics. John Maynard Keynes, the British economist, believed in the private sector but also in a strong government role, especially during dire economic straits. Keynes understood that *demand* from consumers drives an economy; and when consumers don't have a job, an economy will stagnate or worse. So during a cyclical depression, the best response of government is to use government money—even borrowed government money if need be—to put people to work so they'll have money to buy things.

Those expenditures by working-class people—on computers, television sets, clothes, toys, furniture, power tools, and so on—would help restart the economy, which would grow gross domestic product (GDP) and tax revenues, so government would be able to pay back the borrowed money and wean people off of government jobs as private industry picked up the load. (Keynes even suggested that this was such an important principle that it would work if government simply hired one man to dig a hole and another man to fill it back up a week later.)

It worked in the 1930s with federal projects like Roosevelt's Civilian Conservation Corps (CCC), which put 3 million Americans to work on various conservation and natural resources projects; his Works Progress Administration (WPA), which employed millions on public works projects; and an alphabet soup of other "pubic employment" agencies. That same principle—government stimulating the economy through job creation—was working in 2010, albeit anemically, in large part because the stimulus bill was one-third the size it should have been. It was a vindication of Keynesian economics, but nobody knew it outside of political insiders and policy wonks because the stimulus package hadn't been large enough to actually create a net surplus of jobs. Instead it had only stopped the hemorrhaging that had started during the Bush administration with the loss of more than 7 million jobs in less than two years.

So there I was at the White House, listening to the top economist trying to figure out why this "stimulus bill" had not really stimulated much of anything, certainly not good PR for Obama. For example, four days later a front-page headline in the *New York Times* blared "Despite Signs of Recovery, Chronic Joblessness Rises." Among other things, the article reported that more than 6.3 million Americans had been jobless for more than six months, the largest number since government started tracking jobless-ness in 1948, and more than 15 million Americans were jobless in January 2010.[1]

What happened to Keynes? How could hundreds of billions of dollars pumped into the economy fail to create jobs making things that working people could buy? If it worked so well in the 1930s and the 1940s, why did it fail to go beyond just "stopping the bleeding" and move into the net creation of new manufacturing jobs in the United States in the 2010s?

In fact, it hadn't failed. It *did* create millions of jobs—prob-ably tens of millions of jobs. The problem is that they were mostly in China.

The simple fact is that we no longer make computers or TVs or clothes or power tools or toys or pretty much anything in the USA, except military hardware, processed food, and pharmaceu-ticals. So when we "stimulate" our economy by putting money into the pockets of working people, they go to Wal-Mart and buy things made in Asia—creating jobs in *that* part of the world.

So here is the first big way we can reboot the economy: lose our recent fascination—obsession, really—with "free trade," get back to protectionism, and impose tariffs (import taxes) on im-ported consumer goods as we used to do. Let's apply the lessons that our own rich history teaches us. In other words, let's resume the manufacture of consumer goods in the United States, protect these industries from cheap foreign labor, and bring all those jobs back home.

The High Cost of "Free Trade"

During the 1930s none of the "Asian powerhouse economies" had adopted American industrialization strategies, so when Roosevelt put money into workers' pockets and they bought toys or clothes or radios, all of those items were made in Alabama or Connecticut or Michigan. Now they're made in China, which experienced a "labor shortage" in 2009, causing its average wage to increase from $0.80 per hour to $1.14 and its economy to grow by more than 8 percent.[2]

China has been following the lead of Japan, Taiwan, and South Korea during the past half century and has become an industrial powerhouse as a result. And, ironically, each of those countries got its strategy from us: George Washington's Treasury secretary, Alexander Hamilton, proposed it in 1791, and by 1793 most of the parts of his *Report on the Subject of Manufactures* had been instituted as a series of legislative and policy steps.[3]

And it didn't start with Hamilton; he was just building on King Henry VII's "Tudor Plan" of 1485, which turned England from a backwater state with raw wool as its chief export into a major developed state that produced fine clothing and other textile products from wool. He accomplished this by severely restricting the export of wool from England with high export tariffs and restricting the import of finished woolen products with high import tariffs. King Henry learned this from the Dutch. They copied the Romans. And the Romans got it from the Greeks three thousand years ago.

Nonetheless, President Obama continues to follow his predecessors—Bush Jr., Clinton, Bush Sr., and Reagan—in the religious belief that "free trade" will save us all. It's nonsense. "Free trade" is a guaranteed ticket to the poorhouse for any nation, and the evidence is overwhelming. Even the very phrase *free trade* was introduced by Henry VII as something that England should encourage *other* countries to do while *it* maintained protectionism.

The Korean Experience

A more contemporary example of the application of that wisdom can be seen in South Korea. In the 1960s Korea was an undeveloped nation whose major exports were human hair (for wigs) and fish and whose average annual income was around $400 per working family. Today it's a major industrial power with an average annual per capita income of more than $32,000, and it beats the United States in its rate of college attendance, exports, and lifespan. Korea did it by closing its economy and promoting its export industries. A decade earlier Japan had done the same thing. Forty years earlier Germany had done it.

In July 2009, with no evident irony or understanding of how South Korea went about becoming a modern economic powerhouse, President Obama lectured the countries of Africa during his visit to Ghana. As the *New York Times* reported: "Mr. Obama said that when his father came to the United States, his home country of Kenya had an economy as large as that of South Korea per capita. Today, he noted, Kenya remains impoverished and politically unstable, while South Korea has become an economic powerhouse."[4]

In the next day's newspaper, the lead editorial, titled "Tangled Trade Talks," repeated the essence of the mantra of its confused op-ed writer, Thomas L. Friedman, that so-called free trade is the solution to a nation's economic ills. "There are few things that could do more damage to the already battered global economy than an old-fashioned trade war," the *Times* opined. "So we have been increasingly worried by the protectionist rhetoric and policies being espoused by politicians across the globe and in this country."[5] But South Korea did not ride the "free trade" train to success.

South Korean economist Ha-Joon Chang details South Korea's economic ascent in his 2007 book *Bad Samaritans: The Myth of Free Trade and the Secret History of Capitalism*. In 1961 South Korea was as poor as Kenya, with an $82 per capita annual income and many obstacles to economic strength. The country's main exports were primary commodities such as tungsten, fish, and human hair for wigs. That's how the Korean technology giant, Samsung, started—by exporting fish, fruits, and vegetables. Today it's the world's largest conglomerate by revenue ($173 billion in 2008). By throwing out "free trade" and embracing "protectionism" during the 1960s, South Korea managed to do in 50 years what it took the United States 100 years and Britain 150 years to do.[6]

After a military coup in 1961, General Park Chung-hee implemented short-term plans for South Korea's economic development. He instituted the Heavy and Chemical Industrialization program, and South Korea's first steel mill and modern shipyard went into production. South Korea also began producing its own cars and used import tariffs to discourage imports. Electronics, machinery, and chemical plants soon followed—all sponsored or subsidized and tariff-protected by the government. Between 1972 and 1979, the per capita income grew more than five times. In addition, new protectionist slogans were adopted by South Korean citizens. For example, it was viewed as civic duty to report anyone caught smoking foreign cigarettes.

All money made from exports went into developing industry. South Korea enacted import bans, high tariffs, and excise taxes on thousands of products.

In the 1980s South Korea's economy was still far from that of the industrialized West, but the country had built a solid middle class. South Korea's transformation was, to quote Chang, as if "Haiti had turned into Switzerland." This transformation was accomplished through protecting fledgling industries with high tariffs and subsidies and by only gradually opening itself to global competition.

In addition, the government ran or heavily funded many of the larger industries, at least until they were globally competitive. The government ran or regulated the banks and therefore the credit. It controlled foreign exchange and used its currency reserves to import machinery and industrial products. At the same time, the government tightly controlled foreign investment in South Korea and largely ignored enforcement of foreign patent laws. Korea focused on importing basic goods, to fuel and protect its high-tech industries with tariffs and subsidies.

Had South Korea adopted the "free trade" policies espoused by Friedman and the *New York Times,* it would still be exporting human hair.

Another favorite Friedman free-trade example is the success of Toyota's Lexus luxury car, immortalized in his book *The Lexus and the Olive Tree.* But again, the reality is quite different from what Friedman naïvely portrays in his book. In fact, Japan subsidized Toyota not only in its development but even after it failed terribly in the American markets in the late 1950s. In addition, early in Toyota's development, Japan kicked out foreign competitors like General Motors. Thus, because the Japanese government financed Toyota at a loss for roughly 20 years, built high tariff and other barriers to competitive imports, and initially subsidized exports, auto manufacturing was able to get a strong foothold, and we now think of Japanese exports as being synonymous with automobiles.

Founding Father Knows Best

For about 200 years, we understood well the benefits of tariffs, subsidized exports, and protectionist policies in the United States. Had the Founders, like Abraham Lincoln, George Washington, Andrew Jackson, or Ulysses S. Grant, applied for loans from the International Monetary Fund (IMF), they would have been denied: all of them believed in high tariffs and a heavy control of foreign investment and considered "free trade" absurd.

But it was another Founding Father, Alexander Hamilton, who knew best how to spawn American industry to make the country independent and competitive. As the nation's first Treasury secretary, Hamilton submitted his *Report on the Subject of Manufactures* in 1791 to the U.S. Congress, outlining the need for our government to foster new industries through "bounties" (subsidies) and subsequently protect them from foreign imports until they become globally competitive. Additionally, he proposed a road map for American industrial development. These steps included protective tariffs on imports, import bans, subsidies, export bans on selected materials, and the development of product standards. (See "Alexander Hamilton's 11-point Plan for 'American Manufactures'" in the introduction.)

It was this approach of putting America first that our government followed for most of our history, with average tariffs of 30 to 40 percent through the nineteenth and twentieth centuries. There is no denying that it helped turn America into an industrial and economic juggernaut in the midtwentieth century and beyond. The three periods when we radically dropped tariffs—for three years in 1857, for nine years in 1913, and by Reagan in 1987—all were followed by economic disasters, particularly for small American manufacturers.

The post-Reagan era has been particularly destructive to our economy because we not only mostly eliminated the tariffs but we also became "free trade" proponents on the international stage. After Reagan blew out our tariffs in the 1980s and Clinton kicked the door off the hinges with the General Agreement on Tariffs and Trade (GATT), North American Free Trade Agreement (NAFTA), and World Trade Organization (WTO), our average tariffs are now around 2 *percent.* The predictable result has been the hemorrhaging of American manufacturing capacity to those countries that do protect their industries through high import tariffs but allow exports on the cheap—particularly China and South Korea.

The irony is that we have abandoned Hamilton's advice—and our own history—while China, South Korea, Japan, and other nations are following his prescriptions and turning into muscular and prosperous economic entities.

It's high time we relearned Alexander Hamilton's lessons for our nation.

The first third of Hamilton's report deals with Jefferson's objections to it (withdrawn later), which were primarily over the subsidies to industry, as Jefferson in 1791 favored America's being an agricultural rather than an industrial power. After that,

Hamilton gets to the rationale for, and the details of, his 11-point plan to turn America into an industrial power and build a strong manufacturing-based middle class.

First, Hamilton notes that real wealth doesn't exist until somebody makes something. A "service economy" is an oxymoron: if I wash your car in exchange for your mowing my lawn, money is moving around, it's an "economy" of some sort, but no real and lasting wealth is created. Only through manufacturing, when $5 worth of iron ore is converted into a $2,000 car door, or $1 worth of raw wool is converted into a $1,000 suit, is real wealth created. Hamilton also notes that people being paid for creating wealth (manufacturing) creates wages, which are the principal engine of demand that drives an economy. And both come from a generally protectionist foreign-trade policy.

In an early version of Keynesian economics, Hamilton noted that when people make things, they also earn money, which will be used to buy more things, thus creating a real economy with things of real value circulating in it. In addition, Hamilton saw a clear government role in fostering manufacturing, not just in subsidizing it until it could compete on its own but also in crafting a foreign policy that favored the protection of American enterprises. "It is for the United States to consider by what means they can render themselves least dependent," on other nations' manufactures, Hamilton wrote, "on the combinations, right or wrong, of foreign policy."[7]

But there were many voices—the loudest being the young Thomas Jefferson—who argued that instead of becoming an industrial power the United States should remain an agricultural nation. Hamilton believed that both were possible, and there would even be a desirable synergy between the two. He felt that if America wanted to be competitive, it couldn't just leave it to the free market, at least not until homegrown industries were robust enough to compete on their own in the international marketplace.

Government ought to play a role in fostering a strong industrial base, he argued: "To produce the desirable changes, as early as may be expedient, may therefore require the incitement and patronage of government." In fact, Hamilton believed that success was not possible without government. "To be enabled, to contend with success, it is evident that the interference and aid of their own government are indispensable," he wrote.

His reasons were pretty straightforward: it would take government's power to set up a playing field for the game of business where investors who would otherwise be able to make more money overseas would keep their money in the United States. "There are weighty inducements to prefer the employment of capital at home, even at less profit, to an investment of it abroad, though with greater gain," he wrote.

Having provided this overview, Hamilton got right to the meat of the matter—his 11-step plan (see the sidebar in the introduction). It called for government to take an active role in developing its own industry, in discouraging imports through tariffs and prohibitions, in building transportation routes at home for internal trade, and in subsidizing manufacturing until companies become strong enough to compete on their own.

Consider the historical impact of Hamilton's plan, which was adopted in a series of piecemeal legislative steps mostly in 1793: tariffs became so important that they constituted pretty much the only source of revenue for the federal government until the Civil War, and they were the single largest source of federal revenue from then until World War I. And even when the U.S. government grew exponentially in the lead-up to World War II, fully one-third of all federal revenues came from tariffs.

It is only since the Reagan era and subsequently with Bush Sr., Clinton, and then Bush Jr., that we have forsaken tariffs and have been chanting the "free trade" mantra—to our own detriment and destruction. A protectionist approach, including tariffs, is what the USA needs so that it can get back in the game of manufacturing—before it's too late.

Rebooting the Economy

So in my meeting in February 2010 at the White House, I pointed out to the administration economist that when Ronald Reagan came into office, as the result of 190 years of Hamilton's plan, the United States was the world's largest importer of raw materials; the world's largest exporter of finished, manufactured goods; and the world's largest creditor.

After 30 years of Reaganomics, we've completely flipped this upside down: we've become the world's largest exporter of raw materials, the world's largest importer of finished goods, and the world's largest debtor. We now export raw materials to China, and buy from it manufactured goods. And we borrow from China to do it. I pointed out that China's "stimulus package"—about the same size as ours at around $800 billion—could explicitly be spent only on Chinese-made products from Chinese-owned companies employing only Chinese workers. Ditto for the 2009 Japanese version of "Cash for Clunkers," which mandated the purchase of only Japanese cars.

Although no fan of the Reagan revolution, the Obama administration's economic policy team is no fan of protectionism either. Nevertheless, the senior economist at the table reiterated the administration's goal of creating "new jobs" here in the United States.

Well, here's how we can do it.

Create New Jobs Here at Home

First, charge an import tax—a tariff—on goods made overseas that compete with domestic manufacturers, while keeping import taxes low on raw materials that domestic industries need.

Somehow it has become unfashionable in the post-Reagan era to talk about tariffs. An easy way of explaining tariffs is to say, "If there's a dollar's worth of labor in a pair of shoes manufactured in the United States, and you can make the same pair of shoes with twenty cents worth of labor in China, we're going to charge you an eighty-cent tariff when those shoes are imported into the United States. If you can make them with fifty cents of labor in Mexico, our import tariff from Mexico is fifty cents." In short, import duties are used to equalize manufacturing costs and protect domestic industries.

And the tariffs' equalizing effects shouldn't be limited to labor. Products from countries where toxic chemicals can just be poured into rivers (eventually ending up in the oceans we all share) instead of being more expensively disposed of or recycled, should be assessed a tariff to reflect that environmental cost. The same should apply to the way they generate their electricity (for example, using old coal-fired power plants that belch toxins into our air) to manufacture parts for the products.

Second, pull us out of the WTO, NAFTA, CAFTA (Central American Free Trade Agreement), and the rest, and mandate that all purchases made with U.S. taxpayers' dollars be spent on goods and services provided by American workers employed by U.S.-domiciled and -incorporated businesses on American soil. No exceptions. (No more hiring Dubai-based Halliburton, for example.)

Third, have the government support new and emerging industries through tax policy, direct grants, and funding things like the National Institutes of Health, which funds most university research that leads to profitable new drugs for our pharmaceutical companies. In Japan it's the Ministry of Industry and Trade that helped develop the Lexus so beloved by Thomas Friedman. There is no shame in subsidizing our own companies—so long as they show their loyalty to the nation by employing American workers, investing in American enterprises, and not engaging in international business ventures that hurt America.

Then there are other tax incentives and domestic policies to pursue that will benefit the creation of jobs at home. Encourage Americans to save so that there's a strong pool of investment capital for businesses to borrow against and grow. The best way to do this is to offer people an above-the-inflation-rate interest rate on savings. This could easily be accomplished by offering U.S. government savings bonds with a guaranteed rate of return (for example, inflation plus 3 points) and limiting their purchase to people who have a net worth of less than $5 million and selling no more than $1 million per person. This would establish a benchmark against which banks would have to compete, stimulating private banks and credit unions to offer higher returns on savings.

These are bold moves, no doubt, for any president or party to make, but they do have the advantage of pleasing the Tea Party conservative populists as well as the Coffee Party progressive populists. Of course, such protectionist policies would not sit well with some of the multinational conglomerates, whose loyalty is not to America but to their investors and shareholders. A lot of them manufacture products in China or Vietnam and sell them here at a huge profit without giving a damn about the consequences of these actions to American workers.

And these multinational corporations have newfound power, given the recent *Citizens United v. Federal Election Commission* decision of the U.S. Supreme Court (see chapter 10) asserting that even foreign corporations are persons with constitutional protections of things like free speech. Now they can freely carpet-bomb politicians they either love or hate with cash or attack ads during elections. This poses a serious threat to any politician who pushes policies or legislation that is not in the financial interest of the corporations—even if it *is* in the economic interest of the USA.

Whether it was coincidental or consequential, a week after that Supreme Court decision President Obama was backpedaling on many of his criticisms of bankers and other companies who could easily outspend him or any other politician or political party.

And no matter how well the authors and the bloggers I was with at the White House can help President Obama and the Democrats in Congress tell the story of their accomplishments, that ability of corporations to now promote or destroy a politician or political party is a problem that—like our persistent unemployment arising from our loss of manufacturing—is not going to go away on its own. The President and Congress need to do something drastic, like amending the Constitution to say that corporations are not "persons," and reinstituting the trade policies that worked so well from the time of George Washington to, most recently, Harry S. Truman, Dwight D. Eisenhower, John F. Kennedy, Lyndon Baines Johnson, Richard M. Nixon, and Jimmy Carter.

Instead, Obama and the Democrats seem to have joined the Republicans in drinking the Tom Friedman Kool-Aid, and Middle America is looking more and more like Jonestown.

CHAPTER 2

Roll Back the Reagan Tax Cuts

You must pay the price if you wish to secure the blessings.

—Andrew Jackson

W<small>HEN</small> I <small>WAS IN</small> D<small>ENMARK IN</small> 2008 <small>DOING MY RADIO SHOW FOR</small> a week from the Danish Radio studios and interviewing many of that nation's leading politicians, economists, energy experts, and newspaper publishers, one of my guests made a comment that dropped the scales from my eyes.[1]

We'd been discussing taxes on the air and the fact that Denmark has an average 52 percent income-tax rate. I asked him why people didn't revolt at such high taxes, and he smiled and pointed out to me that the average Dane is very well paid, with a minimum wage that equals roughly $18 per hour. Moreover, what Danes get for their taxes (that we don't) is a free college education and free health care, not to mention four weeks of paid vacation each year and notoriety as the happiest nation on earth, according to a major study done by the University of Leicester in the United Kingdom.[2]

But it was once we were off the air that he made the comment that I found so enlightening.

"You Americans are such suckers," he said. "You think that the rules for taxes that apply to rich people also apply to working people, but they don't. When working peoples' taxes go up, their pay goes up. When their taxes go down, their pay goes down. It may take a year or two or three to all even out, but it always works this way—look at any country in Europe. And that rule on taxes is the opposite of how it works for rich people!"

My Danish guest was right. So before we get into the larger consequences of tax increases or tax cuts for the nation's economic health, let's parse this business about what tax increases or cuts mean for the rich and for the not-so-rich.

Unequal Taxation and the Conservative Spin

If a wealthy person earns so much money that he doesn't or can't spend it all each year, when his taxes go down his income after taxes goes up. This is largely because there's little or no relation-ship between what he "needs to live on" and what he's "earning." Somebody living on $1 million per year but earning $5 million after taxes can sock away $4 million in a Swiss bank. If his taxes go up enough to drop his after-tax income to only $3 million per year, he's still living on $1 million per year and socks away only $2 million in the Swiss bank. Although his lifestyle doesn't change, his discretionary income—some call it "disposable" income—goes down when his taxes go up and vice versa.

Most working Americans believe that their taxes and income work in the same way—something the right-wing think tanks and media want everyone to believe. So average Americans tend to support tax cuts because they think they'll have more money in the bank as a result, but if their taxes go up, they'll have less money in the bank. It's pretty intuitive, and over the short term, it's true.

But it never plays out that way. Our own experience—and the experience of the Danes and other Europeans—shows a com-pletely different trend.

Unlike the rich, most working people spend pretty much all of what they earn—their discretionary income is extremely limited and in many cases zero. Savings rates in the United States among working people typically are small—1 to 5 percent. So the take-home pay that people have after taxes—regardless of what the tax rate may be—is pretty much what they live on.

As economist David Ricardo pointed out in 1817 in the "On Wages" chapter of his book *On the Principles of Political Economy and Taxation,* take-home pay is also generally what a person will work for. Employers know this: Ricardo's "Iron Law of Wages" is rooted in the notion that there is a "market" for labor, driven in part by supply and demand.

So, if a worker is earning, for example, a gross salary of $75,000, his 2009 federal income tax would have been about $18,000, leaving him a take-home pay of $57,000. Both he and his employer know that he'll do the job for that $57,000 take-home pay.

So let's take a look at what happens if the government raises income taxes. For our average $75,000-per-year worker, his take-home pay might decrease from $57,000 to $52,000. So, in the short run, increased taxes have an immediate negative effect on him.

But here comes the part the conservatives don't like to talk about. Our own history shows that within a short time—usually between one and three years—that same worker's wages will increase enough to more than compensate for his lost income. Former Federal Reserve Chairman Alan Greenspan used to be hysterical about this effect—he called it "wage inflation"—and the *Wall Street Journal* and other publications would often reference it. It's one reason why as income taxes increasingly hit more and more working people in the United States between the 1950s and 1981, income itself steadily went up, too.

Similarly, when the government enacts a tax cut, working-class people's taxes go down; but sure enough, over time, their wages also go down so their inflation-adjusted take-home pay remains the same.

Consider all the "tax cuts" working people have gotten over the past 30 years, from Reagan, Clinton, and Bush Jr. In each case, within a year or two working people's wages were the same or lower. On the other hand, when working-class people's taxes went up, during the Truman, Eisenhower, Johnson, and Nixon administrations, their wages went up in the following years, too.

We've seen both happen over the past 80 years, over and over again.

When it comes to the rich, though, it is the "top marginal tax rate" that matters most. That marginal tax rate applies to each bracket, and for 2009 taxes it was as follows:

Annual Income	Marginal Tax Rate
Less than $8,350	10%
$8,350 to $33,950	15%
$33,950 to $82,250	25%
$82,250 to $171,550	28%
$171,550 to $372,950	33%
$372,950 and higher	35%

So what happens if that top marginal tax rate goes up from its current 35 percent to, for example, the 1980 rate of 70 percent?

For the more than 120 million American workers who don't earn more than $372,950 annually, it won't mean a thing. But for the tiny handful of millionaires and billionaires who have promoted the Great Tax Con, it will bite hard. And that's why they spend millions to make average working people freak out about increases in the top tax rates.

Taxes as the Great Stabilizer

Beyond fairness, holding back the landed gentry that the Founders worried about—America had no billionaires in today's money until after the Civil War, with John D. Rockefeller being our first—in and of itself is an important reason to increase the top marginal tax rate and to do so now.

Novelist Larry Beinhart was the first to bring this to my attention. He looked over the history of tax cuts and economic bubbles and found a clear relationship between the two. High top marginal tax rates—generally well above 60 percent—on rich people actually stabilize the economy, prevent economic bubbles from forming, prevent the subsequent economic crashes, and lead to steady and sustained economic growth as well as steady and sustained wage growth for working people.[3]

On the other hand, when top marginal rates drop below 50 percent, the opposite happens.

As Beinhart noted, the massive Republican tax cuts of the 1920s (from 73 to 25 percent) led directly to the Roaring Twenties' real estate and stock market bubbles, a temporary boom, and then the crash and Republican Great Depression that started in 1929.

Then, from the 1930s to the 1980s, rates on the very rich went back up into the 70 to 90 percent range. As a result, the economy grew steadily, and for the first time in the history of our nation we went 50 years without a crash or major bank failure. It was also during this period that the American worker's wages increased enough to produce the strongest middle class this nation has ever seen.

Then came Reaganomics.

Taking his cues from the conservative billionaires who fund right-wing think tanks like the Heritage Foundation, Reagan cut top marginal tax rates on the rich from 74 percent to 38 percent. Predictably, there was an immediate surge in the markets—followed by the worst crash since the Great Depression and the failure of virtually the entire nation's savings-and-loan banking system.

Then came Bush Sr., running on his "no new taxes" pledge, who cut taxes once in office; the nation fell into a severe recession while debt soared and wages for working people fell.

During the Bill Clinton era, things stabilized somewhat when he slightly raised taxes on the very rich, but he was followed by

Bush Jr., who cut them again, including cutting taxes on *unearned* income—interest and dividends that people like W, who are born with a trust fund, "earn" as they sit around the pool waiting for the dividend check to arrive in the mail—down to a top rate of 15 percent. That's right, trust fund babies like Bush (and hedge fund billionaires) pay a *maximum* 15 percent federal income tax on their dividend and capital gains income, thanks to the second Bush tax cut.

The result of this surge in easy money for the wealthy, combined with deregulation in the financial markets, was the "froth" Greenspan worried about that led us straight into the Second Republican Great Depression in 2008.

The math is pretty simple. When the über-rich are heavily taxed, economies prosper and wages for working people steadily rise. When taxes for the rich are cut, working people suffer and economies turn into casinos.

How They Did It

So why is it that Americans have come to believe that tax cuts are good for everyone? The answer is that for decades now the über-rich have relentlessly spent money to make Americans believe that lower taxes are the answer to all of America's problems. They've done this partly through the media they own and partly through funding "think tanks" that legitimize their Great Tax Con.

Richard Mellon Scaife, a Pittsburgh native and heir to the Mellon family businesses, is a conservative billionaire who carries the title of publisher of the *Pittsburgh Tribune-Review,* the second-fiddle newspaper to that city's larger daily, the *Pittsburgh Post-Gazette.* Although daily newspapers generally have not been faring well lately, Scaife's *Tribune-Review* is a ridiculously expensive enterprise, given its paltry circulation of 50,000.

According to a 2007 report in the *Post-Gazette,* based on Scaife's divorce filings, his ex-wife contended that the *Tribune-*

Review "should be considered a hobby or personal cause rather than a business investment because the paper has lost $20 million to $30 million annually since it began publishing in 1992."[4]

His ex-wife had it right—the newspaper *is* a "personal cause" for Scaife.

If you do the math, you come up with more than $300 million that Scaife has lost on the newspaper. The Internal Revenue Service (IRS) considers an activity a business (instead of a hobby) if there is "a reasonable expectation" of earning a profit and if it makes a profit in at least three of the past five years (although they've never gone after Scaife on this; as Leona Helmsley famously said, "Only the little people pay taxes").

Scaife is not alone among billionaires flushing money down such news operations. As my friend and colleague Cenk Uygur of *The Young Turks* pointed out in a Daily Kos diary in July 2009, billionaire Rupert Murdoch loses $50 million per year on the *New York Post,* billionaire Philip Anschutz loses around $5 million per year on the *Weekly Standard,* and billionaire Sun Myung Moon has lost $2 to $3 *billion* on the *Washington Times.*[5]

So why are these guys willing to lose so much money funding conservative media? Why do they bulk-buy every right-wing book that comes out to push it to the top of the bestseller list and then give away the copies to "subscribers" to their Web sites and publications? Why do they fund to the tune of hundreds of millions of dollars per year right-wing think tanks and training programs and lobbying organizations?

The answer is pretty straightforward: they do it because it buys them respectability and gets their con job out there. And one of their most important goals is lower taxes—for millionaires and billionaires like themselves.

Scaife, for instance, has used the various family foundations he oversees to fund conservative causes over the years to the tune of hundreds of millions of dollars, including more than $20 million to just the Heritage Foundation. All you have to do to see how influential Heritage has been is to read its own propaganda. When President Reagan took office in 1981, Heritage dropped a 1,100-page tome titled *Mandate for Leadership* on his desk, which he promptly handed out to his entire cabinet. Among its achievements over the years, Heritage lists this under 1981:

> **A tax cut revolution.**
>
> Heritage's *Mandate for Leadership* called for "An across-the-board reduction in marginal personal income tax rates in each bracket of about 10 percent in 1981, with similar rate reductions in 1982 and 1983." The Reagan administration not only followed *Mandate*'s lead, but it appointed Heritage's Norman Ture, the *Mandate* author who penned the chapter on tax policy, as treasury secretary for tax and economic affairs—a new position suggested by *Mandate*. The tax cut that eventually passed—a marginal rate reduction of 25 percent over three years—wiped out America's economic "malaise," producing the biggest economic boom in U.S. history.[6]

This conveniently ignores the fact that the tax cuts also resulted in the tripling of the federal deficit during the Reagan years, among other things. In January 2005, Heritage issued a much shorter, 156-page *Mandate for Leadership* and had this to say about it:[7]

> The original version, published in 1980, was written for a new administration just gaining widespread support for its ideas. Dubbed the "bible" of the Reagan White House by the *Washington Post,* it provided a step-by-step guide to how to transform conservative principles into government policy.
>
> "Today, those principles are well established in Washington, well accepted by American voters and well understood everywhere in terms of how they translate into policy," [President Edwin] Feulner said.

Heritage is but one example of the ways that the rich succeed in influencing public policy, especially tax policy. One hears a constant drumbeat emanating from Heritage and other conservative think tanks to keep taxes low. And the conservative media that these same funders—billionaires like Scaife, Murdoch, Anschutz—own and finance are echoing those messages.

Even though William Kristol's publication, the *Weekly Standard,* is a money-losing joke (with only 85,000 subscribers), his association with the publication is enough to get him on TV talk shows whenever he wants and even a column with the *New York Times* for a year. Similarly, the money-losing *Washington Times* catapulted Tony Blankley to TV stardom. And of course, Murdoch's Fox "News" blares the anti-income-tax message 24/7.

One way in which the think tanks and the conservative media con the American public is to conflate income taxes for the rich with income taxes for everyone else. And this is the crux of the con job. When Bill Clinton proposed tax increases in 1993, think tanks like Heritage and Cato immediately opposed them with their myths about the negative consequences of tax increases. Here's what a Heritage "analyst" wrote then:[8]

> Proponents of raising taxes argue that the federal budget cannot be balanced without a tax hike. They argue, too, that tax increases will make the tax code fairer. Some even claim that tax increases will encourage economic growth by reducing the need for federal borrowing.
>
> Raising taxes, however, would be a political and economic mistake, regardless of who pays and what taxes are increased. If history is any guide, higher taxes will fuel additional federal spending....
>
> Higher taxes will shrink the tax base and reduce tax revenues.... In each case, proponents of the hike claimed that the deficit would decline. But in each case, the deficit rose the following year.

That "analysis" failed to point out that the federal budget has pretty much grown every year since the founding of the republic and that between the growth of both our population and our economy, and the effect of inflation, government expenditures go up every year regardless of tax policy.

Weeks later the Cato Institute, also funded heavily by wealthy right-wing supporters, echoed the opposition to the Clinton tax increases in a piece by Bruce Bartlett, titled "The Futility of Raising Tax Rates," making a special effort to connect taxes for the rich with taxes for everyone else:[9]

> The Clinton plan, therefore, is based on false premises and is unlikely to achieve the goal of increasing the tax burden on the wealthy. It will probably lead, instead, to higher taxes on the poor and the middle class, as higher revenues from the rich fail to materialize. In the end, the burden of higher taxes must fall largely on the middle class because that is where the bulk of income is. Thus, maintaining a low top tax rate is the best way to ensure that tax rates remain reasonable for those with low and moderate incomes.

These anti-tax messages have been delivered by clever language crafted by right-wing message experts like Frank Luntz and others so that terms like *tax relief* and *tax burden* have become household words. In the end, low tax rates, as we saw earlier, only keep the superwealthy—Moon and Murdoch and Scaife and Anschutz (and others)—richer than you or I could ever even imagine being. For these rich right-wing funders, the cash spent on money-losing media enterprises really is a "personal cause"—an investment that pays back by saving them millions in taxes each year.

It's time we roll back the Reagan tax cuts that slashed the top 74 percent rate on millionaires and billionaires down into the low 30s. Let's increase the top marginal tax rate and eliminate stock options as a form of executive compensation. This will go a long way toward stabilizing our economy and improving wages for lower- and middle-income Americans.

Taxing the very rich (who use only a small percentage of their income to "buy" things, stashing most of it in Swiss bank accounts) also supports working people in getting decent wages. When income above $3 million per year (from *all* sources) is taxed at 74 percent, as it was from 1964 to 1983, or at 91 percent, as it was from 1931 to 1964, CEO pay tends to drop down to around 30 times the pay of a company's most lowly paid employees (as it was in the United States from 1932 until the mid-1980s and as it is in virtually every other nation of the world with similarly high top marginal tax rates). Worker wages are healthy, and a landed gentry superwealth class doesn't emerge to threaten democratic institutions and mess with politics in ways that purely advantage only themselves. In other words, roll back the Reagan tax cuts.

The Stock Option Problem

My radio show has a mission statement. We don't say it on the air, as it sounds a bit pompous, but it's the metric against which we measure our work: *Saving the world, by awakening one person at a time.* During the 1980s, when I was CEO of an advertising agency[10] in Atlanta, our mission statement was to help people communicate, to make better and more open companies. Before that, in 1983, I started a travel company[11] that hit the front page of the *Wall Street Journal* the next year and has conducted around a quarter billion dollars in business since then, and its mission statement was to help people better understand the world by traveling through it. And in 1978 my wife and I started a community for abused children[12] in New Hampshire, with a clear mission statement: *Saving the world, one child at a time.*

For most of American history, businesses—for-profit and nonprofit—had mission statements that were broader than simply serving the interests of shareholders and CEOs and referred instead to the long-term interests of the company, its workers, and its customers.

Economics author Barry C. Lynn noted that "by the 1950s managers were wont to present themselves as 'corporate stewards' whose job was to serve 'stockholders, employees, customers, and the public at large.'"[13] In other words, besides the stockholders, there are also the workers, the customers, and the general public, who are crucial to the long-term well-being of the corporation itself. CEOs actually rose through the ranks of the business and felt loyal to the companies they ran. They'd often started in the mailroom as a 20-year-old and fully expected to retire with a comfortable pension, the company in the good hands of one of their younger protégé vice presidents, who was working his or her way to that CEO status.

That corporate mentality and mission was generally true all the way until the 1980s. But in the early Reagan years, something changed dramatically, and it's devastated the American corporate landscape.

First, President Reagan effectively stopped enforcing the Sherman Antitrust Act of 1890, a law that effectively prevented cartels and monopolies and large corporations from dominating the markets. The Reagan administration's backing off from enforcement of the act led to an explosion of mergers and acquisitions, buy-outs, greenmail, forced mergers, and other aggregations of previously competitive or totally unrelated companies. The big got bigger, the midsized got acquired or crushed, and the space in which small entrepreneurs could start and flourish nearly vanished.

But what followed this was even worse. Starting back in the 1930s, a particularly toxic form of economic thinking—some would argue sociopathic economic thinking—began to take hold, some of it propelled by theories developed at the Chicago School of Economics by Milton Friedman (who would later serve as an economic adviser to Reagan). By the 1980s that economic thinking had undergone several mutations, and the one that has hit America the hardest is the notion that every business in the nation has a single mission statement: *maximize shareholder value and dividends.*

The theory behind this was that in a modern corporation the role of the CEO and the executive-level workers is to do whatever is best for the shareholders.

To provide the incentive to CEOs and senior executives to "think like a shareholder," tax and accounting rules were both changed and used in the 1980s to actually turn CEOs into more shareholder than employee. This was done by moving huge chunks of their compensation from payroll (cash) into stocks and stock options (the right to buy stock in the future at current prices and then quickly sell it for a profit). Although a CEO like Stephen J. Hemsley of UnitedHealth Group made an annual salary of $13.2 million in 2007, and $3.2 million in 2009 (a year when CEO pay in the health-care industry was under a lot of scrutiny), he was awarded more than $744 million worth of stock options during the few years he was CEO. His predecessor, William "Dollar Bill" McGuire, was paid more than $1.7 *billion* in stock options for his previous decade of work as CEO.[14]

Such compensation packages are now relatively common across corporate America, having created a new CEO aristocracy as well as a totally different business climate from the way America was before Reagan.

Besides the fact that such stock option deals are extremely lucrative for these executives without making their salaries seem sky high, they have another somewhat insidious effect. Because CEOs are now first and foremost stockholders, every decision is grounded in and colored by the question *Will it immediately increase the price of my stock and the amount of the dividend income it pays?*

Left in the dust are questions like *What is best for this company's long-term survival?* and *What is best for the communities in which we do business?* Stock values are best increased by ruthlessly slashing costs (cutting employees, outsourcing to cheap-labor countries, and cutting corners in production) and increasing revenues (buying up competitors to create monopoly markets so price competition is minimized).

What's more, the money these CEOs and executives make from the sale of the stocks they own or from the dividends those stocks pay is subject to an income tax of only 15 percent (as opposed to the 35 percent top marginal tax rate), the result of the Bush tax cuts. No wonder the rich are getting richer, the jobs are going abroad, and average workers are just plain old out of luck.

Shrink the Government by Raising Taxes

From 1985 until 2008, William A. Niskanen was the chairman of the Cato Institute, a libertarian think tank, and before 1985 he was chairman of Reagan's Council of Economic Advisers and a key architect of Reaganomics. He figured out something that would explode Reagan's head if he were still around. Looking at the 24-year period from 1981 to 2005, when the great experiment of cutting taxes (Reagan) then raising them (Bush Sr. and Clinton) then cutting them again (Bush Jr.) played out, Niskanen saw a clear trend: when taxes go up, government shrinks, and when taxes go down, government gets bigger.

Consider this: You have a clothing store and you offer a "50 percent off" sale on everything in the store. What happens? Sales go up. Do it for a few years and you'll even need to hire more workers and move into a larger store because sales will continue to rise if you're selling below cost. "But won't the store go broke?" you may ask. Not if it's able to borrow unlimited amounts of money and never—or at least not for 20 years or more—pay it back.

That's what happens when we have unfunded tax cuts. Taxpayers get government services—from parks and schools to corporate welfare and crop subsidy payments—at a lower cost than they did before the tax cuts. And, like with anything else, lower cost translates into more demand.

This is why when Reagan cut taxes massively in the 1980s, he almost doubled the size of government: there was more demand for that "cheap government" because nobody was paying for it. And, of course, he ran up a massive debt in the process, but that was invisible because the Republican strategy, called "two Santa Clauses," is to run up government debt when in office and spend the money to make the economy seem good, and then to scream about the debt and the deficit when Democrats come into office. So while Reagan and W were exploding our debt, there wasn't a peep from the right or in the media; as soon as a Democrat was elected (Clinton and Obama), both the right-wingers and the corporate media became hysterical about the debt.

And when Clinton raised taxes so that people actually started paying the true cost of government (a balanced budget as in the years 1999 and 2000), they concluded that they didn't need as many services, so government actually shrank—in terms of both cost and the number of federal employees.

Then Bush Jr. comes into office and goes back to Reaganomics and again cuts taxes and puts the cost on the national credit card, and, bingo, he presides over the largest increase in the size and the cost of government in the history of our republic.

The Reaganomics theory was that people would use less government when they saw the huge deficits that use of government during times of low taxes was racking up, but that's not what happened. Instead, people and businesses ignored the deficit and went shopping for discounted government.

Running the numbers through a fine-toothed comb, Cato's Niskanen was even able to determine the exact tipping point for taxes and demand for government services: 19 percent of GDP. Whenever taxes were above that point (FDR to Carter and during the Clinton years), government grew more slowly than the rest of the economy or even shrank. Whenever taxes were below 19 percent of GDP, government grew in size and spending (usually military but others as well) like a fat man at a pie-eating contest.

"I would like to be proven wrong," Niskanen told *Atlantic Monthly* writer Jonathan Rauch. And Rauch noted, "The way to limit the growth of government is to force politicians, and therefore voters, to pay for all the government they use—not to give them a discount." And that means raising taxes to a point above 19 percent of GDP. "Voters will not shrink Big Government until they feel the pinch of its true cost," Rauch wrote.[15]

Of course this is *very bad news* for people who want to put Reagan's picture on the $50 bill and reshape Roosevelt's face into Reagan's on Mount Rushmore, which is probably why the former chairman of Cato's report on the issue is buried in an obscure part of its Web site and the only significant coverage his discovery ever got was Rauch's article.

But it comports with both common sense and a generation of tax tables. Reagan and Bush Jr. cut taxes, leading to a bloated government and huge debts. Clinton increased taxes, which cut demand for (and thus the size of) government and let him begin to pay down the debt. If "conservatives" really want "small government," they should be talking about putting the guy they call Slick Willy's picture on the 50 instead of Ronnie's.

Reverse and Roll Back

If we want to have long-term economic stability and if we want to have fairness in our tax policy, it is quite clear what we have to do. We have to first undo the damage done by the right-wing think tanks and media, funded by the Scaifes, the Murdochs, the Anschutzes, and the Moons, and get Americans to see taxes not as a burden but as both the admission price to civil society and investments in our nation's future.

For too long the über-rich have spent hundreds of millions to make sure phrases like *tax burden* and *tax relief* have become embedded in the national consciousness, so today people have come to think of taxes as inherently bad. Based on that assumption, the über-rich have also convinced working people that they should throw out of office any politicians who are willing to raise taxes on the rich. (Because there were no right-wing think tanks at the time, Americans applauded rather than screamed about Woodrow Wilson's and Herbert Hoover's raising taxes on rich people above 80 percent.)

So we have to help Americans realize that "no new taxes" is a mantra that is meaningful to the very rich but largely hurts average working people.

Only when the current generation relearns the economic and tax lessons well known by the generation (now dying off) that came of age in the 1930s through the 1960s will this become politically possible. Americans need to learn what Europeans know about income taxes—that they really matter only to the rich.

We need to remind people that it was not that long ago when we had the rich paying top marginal tax rates of 70 percent (at the start of the Reagan years); and if we want to go further back, we used to have top marginal tax rates above *90 percent* in the Eisenhower years. Our current tax rates and the antitax fever are the result of relentless right-wing propaganda that began during the so-called Reagan revolution and has continued ever since.

If we really want our country to recover its financial footing, we must roll back the Reagan tax cuts that took the top marginal rate from above 70 percent down into the 30 percent range. To stop the "casino economy" that always emerges when the very highest-income people are allowed to keep whatever they can get, regardless of how they got it (so long as it's legal), there has to be a collective notion of "how rich is too rich for society to afford" and income above that rate is taxed at the old 70 to 90 percent rate.

In addition to rolling back the Reagan tax cuts so that millionaires and billionaires have little incentive to plunder their companies and slash (or export) their workforces, we must also ban the use of stock options as a form of compensation for top corporate executives. This will shift the focus of CEOs and senior managers from stock price and dividends (a focus that has de-stroyed numerous companies, from Enron to Lehman Brothers to BP) to the long-term health of the company itself.

If we want to keep the stock options as compensation, we must at the least tax those stock options at the same top marginal tax rates as the salaries of the rich by considering capital gains as ordinary income.

We have a lot of educating to do. And so long as the right-wing machine of the über-rich continues to "lose" (i.e., "invest") millions of dollars a year in their ongoing disinformation cam-paign, it's going to require all of us reciting the mantra: "Roll back the Reagan tax cuts!"

CHAPTER **3**

Stop Them from Eating My Town

Unless you become more watchful in your states and check the spirit of monopoly and thirst for exclusive privileges you will in the end find that...the control over your dearest interests has passed into the hands of these corporations.

—Andrew Jackson

THERE IS A HUGE DIFFERENCE BETWEEN A MALL FULL OF CHAIN stores or a big-box retailer, and a downtown area full of small, locally owned businesses. The transition from the latter to the former is what's destroying local communities on the one hand and creating mind-boggling wealth for a very few very large corporations and multimillionaire CEOs on the other. Here's how it works.

As I noted in my book *Unequal Protection*,[1] when I shop in downtown Montpelier, Vermont, and buy a pair of pants, for example, at the Stevens Clothing Store on Main Street, at the end of the day the store's owner, Jack Callahan, takes his proceeds down to the Northfield Savings Bank and deposits them. From Stevens, I walk next door to Bear Pond Books and buy today's newspaper, a magazine, and a copy of Thomas Paine's *Rights of Man*, a book that is as fascinating today as when it was first written in 1791.

At the end of the day, Bear Pond's manager, Linda Leehman, will take my money down to the Chittenden Bank and deposit it.

From Bear Pond I go to one of the dozen or so local restaurants and exchange some of my cash for a good meal. At day's end that cash, too, will end up in one of Montpelier's local banks.

The next day Montpelier's banks are richer by my purchases, as are Stevens, Bear Pond, and the restaurant. If my daughter, a Web designer, wanted to start her own design firm in an office on Main Street (or from her home), she could visit one of those banks, and, if her credit was good, they could loan her some of the money that was deposited with them the night before from the townspeople's purchases.

If her work is good, Stevens or Bear Pond or the restaurant may decide they want to hire her to design their Web site, using the profits they made from my—and others'—purchases to pay for her work. She'll put her money into the local bank, increasing its deposits available for local lending. Thus, by keeping money within the community, the community grows. This is how communities in America and most of the rest of the world have historically grown.

Consider, though, if my shopping trip had been to a mall full of chain stores or to a national superstore. Strict management of cash flow is the name of the game for such businesses, and some of them make deposits several times a day. But the money stays in town for only a day at best.

Every night, all around America, buttons are pushed that— like vampires draining blood from sleeping people—drain cash away from local communities, most of it never to be seen in town again.

At McDonald's, Wal-Mart, Chili's, Home Depot, and a hundred other national and international chains, local branches spend the entire day selling products made or grown far away and shipped over land or sea. Local customers who earned money locally buy these products every day. Although the companies pay a small amount of their revenue back in local taxes and payroll and services, most of it is sucked up nightly into each company's headquarters bank in Chicago or Little Rock or New York or wherever it may be. And most of that money never returns to the local community.

This is how you destroy local communities; it's the opposite of a healthy economy.

Clearly, we need to reverse this trend and stop the corporate Godzillas from tearing up our local towns and local economies. First, let's take away all the local, state, and federal government incentives and subsidies that these chain operations feed on and which are not usually available to local small businesses. Second, enact measures to stop multinationals from evading U.S. taxes by moving their operations and assets to low-tax countries, and break up the giant trusts that have come to dominate every aspect of our economy. Third, implement and promote policies—through federal agencies such as the Small Business Administration—that provide help and know-how as well as financial incentives to small, independent, local businesses.

In Praise of Inefficiency

This homogenization of stores and restaurants and banks across America is a recent phenomenon; it was not the case for the first 200 years or so of our nation's history.

Other countries are wary of making such stupid blunders.

India, for instance, has a complex of national and local laws that functionally makes it illegal for a business or person to own multiple retail locations anywhere in the country. Thus, while the retail sector accounts for a whopping 14 percent of GDP, 98 percent of the stores are what economists label "unorganized"—owned by single families or businesses. (There is tremendous pressure right now from international corporate oligarchs—being led by Wal-Mart and Microsoft—to change these Indian laws.)

The result is that every neighborhood in every city, every town, and every village in India is filled with small mom-and-pop stores: small grocery stores, small hardware stores, small electronics stores, small music stores, small bookstores, small shoe stores—and on and on through the whole "butcher, baker, and candlestick maker" realm of retail. All locally owned, almost all family owned, for generations.

It's also how America looked from its founding until Reagan stopped enforcing the Sherman Antitrust Act. Shopping centers, strip malls, retail downtown areas, rural country stores—all were mostly family or small-business owned.

This local ownership of small businesses is relatively inefficient. India right now has "the highest shop density in the world" at "11 outlets for every 1,000 people." And that inefficiency is just the way most Indians like it. Products are locally sold and locally consumed—often by people who locally produced them. It is revealing that India has roughly 11 million retail outlets, with 96 percent of them less than 500 square feet in size, and America has fewer than 1 million retail outlets, but they are, in sales, 13 times the size of the Indian market.[2]

That "inefficiency" in the Indian market also means that local money stays in local economies. A local purchase from a local store goes into the pocket of a local shop owner, who deposits the money in a local bank, where it can be loaned out to local people to buy local homes. The local business is also buying products locally to sell and is supporting services like accounting, cleaning, and maintenance. These local businesses in turn keep and spend their money locally.

The result of this "inefficiency" is a nation full of economically healthy local communities and healthy local small businesses.

But when the economic theorists and the big corporations behind the so-called Reagan revolution surveyed the American retail landscape in the early 1980s, they looked at those healthy businesses the way a cancer cell looks at the rest of the body—wide open and ready for a takeover.

In the worldview of Ayn Rand and Milton Friedman, everybody in the world is motivated purely by "self-interest." There are the "smart" people pursuing their own self-interest (also known as "the rich") and the "lazy" people pursuing their own self-interest by using an instrument of force (government regulations, minimum-wage laws, collective bargaining laws, and the like) to extract wealth from the "smart" people for themselves. These latter people are labeled by Randians and Friedmanites as "parasites" or "moochers."

When Reagan stopped enforcing the Sherman Antitrust Act, the result was an explosion of mergers and acquisitions by the "smart" people. Small- and medium-sized businesses were eaten alive by giant behemoths. Mom-and-pop shops went out of business left and right, as did small manufacturing and support companies. All were replaced by national chains, which brought in products from out of town, outsourced their accounting and other back-office work to national headquarters, and every night vacuumed up all the cash they'd collected locally.

They were highly efficient and highly profitable, and the result is a now-unhealthy American retail economy dominated by a few dozen major corporations doing business under thousands of names. Entrepreneurialism has largely vanished from the American landscape; the country of innovation and invention has become the country of imported new gadgets and big-box retailers.

Teddy the Trustbuster

This is only the second time in American history that we've faced such a concentration of wealth and power, of business and money, and of the political control that flows from it; and this is the first time it's been extended to the retail sector.

The previous time was in the late 1800s, when John Pierpont Morgan came to dominate most of the American business landscape (it was called "Morganizing" back then), competing with a handful of oligarchs like John D. Rockefeller and Andrew Carnegie. When Theodore Roosevelt became president in 1901, he set out to break up these cartels, earning himself the moniker "Teddy the Trustbuster."

Today we need a new trustbuster. Clinton and the Bushes refused to go back to enforcing the Sherman Act and other similar laws, both leaving in place and advancing the agenda of the Rand/Friedman corporatists of the Reagan revolution. Obama has made tentative noises about enforcing the Sherman Act but has taken no serious actions.

Monopoly started out as a game invented by Elizabeth Magie and patented in 1904 (she sold her patent to Parker Brothers in 1935 for $500, and they incorporated it into the modern Monopoly game, which was patented that year by Charles Darrow[3]). Magie, who was a Quaker and a political activist, wanted to create a way to inform the average person of how concentration of property ownership and aggregation of rents over time would lead to the concentration of wealth in a few hands, with the rest of the population experiencing widespread poverty.

But over the years, that lesson has been long lost, and players simply enjoy the challenge of buying up every business and property available and, through the monopoly ownership of all businesses and rents, bleeding every other player into poverty.

Today people like Mitt Romney and T. Boone Pickens play the game in the real world, impoverishing real people and destroying real businesses while taking all the cash they can for themselves.

America needs a new Teddy Roosevelt to break up the modern-day monopolists and return opportunity and wealth to local communities and small businesses.

Corporate Welfare

As major corporations are dominating our consumer markets and destroying local economies, they are also doing everything in their power to avoid paying their fair share of the taxes, on the one hand, and to get local and state governments to subsidize their operations, on the other.

A *Forbes* magazine report in April 2010 showed the extent of the scandal and how major U.S.-based multinationals have used an array of complicated tax loopholes and accounting methods to evade paying income taxes in the United States and instead move their tax responsibilities to offshore tax havens:[4]

> The most egregious example is General Electric. Last year the conglomerate generated $10.3 billion in pretax income, but ended up owing nothing to Uncle Sam. In fact, it recorded a tax benefit of $1.1 billion. Avoiding taxes is nothing new for General Electric. In 2008 its effective tax rate was 5.3%; in 2007 it was 15%. The marginal U.S. corporate rate is 35%....
>
> But it's the tax benefit of overseas operations that is the biggest reason why multinationals end up with lower tax rates than the rest of us. It only makes sense that multinationals "put costs in high-tax countries and profits in low-tax countries," says Scott Hodge, president of the Tax Foundation.

The fact that multinationals avoid paying taxes in the United States and even move assets overseas to do so is a clear sign of their loyalty—or rather their lack thereof—to their host country. Another such sign is that even within the United States these companies suck up more tax revenues than they contribute.

As I noted in my book *Unequal Protection,* Paul Hawken, author of *The Ecology of Commerce,* found data in the early 1990s indicating that the nation's corporations were net consumers, rather than producers, of tax monies. Several recent books on corporate welfare point to similar trends and conclusions, although hard data are difficult to come by because the statistics necessary to compile it are spread across literally thousands of separate local, state, and federal government agencies and their reports. "It was almost certainly the case, when I did my initial research in 1992," Hawken told me, "that the nation's corporations took more out of the economy in tax dollars than they pay in."[5]

For example, in 2001 the Boeing Company illustrated how much power it has in the economy. It announced that it would relocate its corporate headquarters from Seattle and then played the offers of three cities against one another. By the time the decision was announced on May 10, 2001, that Boeing chose Chicago, the New York Times reported that the winning destination had "promised tax breaks and incentives that could total $60 million" to seal the deal.[6] Making matters worse for the government was the fact that Boeing enjoyed negative income-tax rates of –18.8 percent from 2001 to 2003.[7]

This is far from rare. According to a report from the Cato Institute, businesses in America receive direct tax subsidies of more than $75 billion annually.[8] That equates to every household in America paying a $750 annual subsidy to corporations, according to Dr. David C. Korten, author and former faculty member of the Harvard Graduate School of Business.[9]

The way that this happens clearly illustrates the consequences of unrestrained "freedom of expression" in the halls of a government that was designed to serve the public good. In a situation that is reminiscent of the charter-mongering era, companies can once again be aggressive in getting local governments to offer tax breaks that are never offered for local, small businesses. All of the following have the effect of cash taken out of human pockets and put into corporate ones:

- In Louisiana a multinational chemical company was given a $15 million tax break.[10]

- In Ohio $2.1 billion worth of business property was taken off the tax rolls, leaving public schools struggling to find resources because they depend most on the now-eviscerated property-tax revenues.*

- New York State companies had, from just 1991 to 1992, "earned" $242 million in tax credits and held $938 million in "unused" tax credits they could "use" in future years to avoid paying an equal amount in corporate income taxes on profits.[11]

- Alabama offered $153 million to a German automobile company to build a factory there, an amount equal to about $200,000 per job created.[12]

- Illinois gave a national retail chain $240 million in land and tax breaks to keep it from moving out of state.[13]

- The state of Indiana borrowed millions from its citizens by a bond issue and gave that money as an "upfront cash subsidy," along with other grants and tax breaks that totaled $451 million, to an airline to build a maintenance facility.[14]

- Pennsylvania gave a Norwegian transnational corporation $235 million in economic incentives to build a shipyard, an amount that cost the state, according to *Time* magazine, $323,000 per job.[15]

- New York City gave tax breaks of $235 million, $98 million, and $97 million to three corporations to keep them from moving to New Jersey, and $25 million to a media

---

*Noreena Hertz notes in *The Silent Takeover* (London: Heinemann, 2001) that "beneficiaries of Ohio's 'corporate welfare' included Spiegel, Wal-Mart, and Consolidated Stores Corporation, all of which were absolved from property taxes....As one school treasurer put it, 'Kids get hurt and stockholders get rich.'"

corporation to keep it in town. (Few of these breaks created any new jobs anywhere.) Says the *New York Times,* "Since Mr. Giuliani took office in 1994, he has provided 34 companies with tax breaks and other incentives totaling $666.7 million."[16]

- Kentucky gave nearly $140 million to two steel manufacturers—more than $350,000 per job created.[17]

- In Louisiana over a 10-year period, just the top 10 corporations getting breaks (there were others) received $836 million to "create jobs." *Time* magazine did the math and found that the cost to the state's taxpayers *per job created* among those 10 ranged from $900,000 to $29 million.[18]

- The state of Michigan created the Michigan Economic Growth Authority (MEGA), which as of 1999 had awarded more than $900 million in tax breaks and grants to corporations, costing Michigan taxpayers, according to the Mackinac Center for Public Policy, $40,000 per job created or moved from other states into Michigan.[19]

In almost every case, benefits to one community were subtracted from another. "No new jobs are created in the process" of most of these sorts of tax breaks, according to former U.S. Secretary of Labor Robert B. Reich, quoted in the *New York Times.* "They're merely moved around. Meanwhile, the public spends a fortune subsidizing these companies. But there's no way that mayors or governors can withstand the heat once a major company announces it is thinking about leaving."[20]

Break the Tax-avoidance Corporate Cycle

So how do we stop multinationals from squeezing major subsidies out of local and state governments to move their operations there—or sometimes simply to stay in their town or state (and threaten to move elsewhere if they are not offered subsidies)?

Withhold Federal Funds

Senator Bernie Sanders, independent from Vermont, suggested a simple solution on my radio show in 2008: "Just pass a law denying federal highway matching funds to any state that participates" in these efforts by corporations to play one state against another.

Because federal highway funds are vital to every state just to keep the roads functioning, the federal government has a long history of threatening to withhold them to coerce desired behavior from the states without actual mandates that may violate the Tenth Amendment. A good example is how Jimmy Carter cut our oil consumption nationwide in the late 1970s by telling states that if they allowed a speed limit above 55 miles per hour (mph), their federal highway funds would be cut: within a year every state in the nation had new signs up proclaiming a 55 mph limit.

So denying federal highway funds to local and state governments that offer huge cash incentives to businesses to move or to stay is really a simple solution and one that needs to be made into law today to stop them from eating your town next!

Close the Tax Loopholes

Another way to stop multinationals from evading taxes in the United States is to close the loopholes that allow them to, for instance, not pay the U.S. tax rate on overseas earnings. The Obama administration has made some noises about doing this.

Under current law, if I give a speech in Australia and earn $10,000, it is taxed by the IRS as earned income. On the other hand, if a multinational corporation earns income in Australia and keeps it in an office there, the IRS can't touch it. Our tax laws should be changed back to the way they were decades ago so that U.S.-incorporated corporations have to report and pay tax on *all* their income, regardless of where it's earned, so they don't have an incentive to move their operations—and keep their profits—overseas.

And if a corporation wants to change its nation of incorporation from the United States to, as in the case of now-Dubai-based Halliburton spin-off KBR, the Cayman Islands (to avoid paying corporate income taxes in the United States), the entire corporate management and their offices should be required to *move* to the nation of incorporation. Or, more simply, just require that any corporation whose principal operations and management are domiciled in the United States must also be incorporated in this nation and pay taxes here. It's frankly embarrassing to the United States that trillions of dollars spent during the Bush and Obama administrations for the wars in Iraq and Afghanistan went to corporations that didn't pay income taxes here on their profits because they reincorporated overseas. Taxpayers are subsidizing tax cheats!

Encourage Entrepreneurialism

Finally, if we as a nation truly believe in entrepreneurship—the very thing that made America an economic success—we need to proactively encourage and provide help and incentives to small businesses.

In the waning year of his presidency in 1932, Herbert Hoover started the Reconstruction Finance Corporation (RFC) to float loans for companies that were falling into bankruptcy because so many banks were on the edge of failing that nobody could borrow money. The RFC continued through the Republican Great Depression years of the 1930s and the war years of the 1940s and eventually inspired the Dwight Eisenhower administration in 1953 to create the Small Business Administration (SBA). The theory by that time was that the economy was solid enough that big and medium-sized businesses could stand on their own but that small businesses still needed some support.

As the Web site for the SBA itself notes, in its history of the day:

> In the Small Business Act of July 30, 1953, Congress created the Small Business Administration, whose function was to "aid, counsel, assist and protect, insofar as is possible, the interests of small business concerns." The charter also stipulated that the SBA would ensure small businesses a "fair proportion" of government contracts and sales of surplus property.[21]

Over time the definition of "small" changed over and over again, and bigger and bigger businesses figured out ways to game the SBA by spinning off new, "small" divisions or simply by lobbying to reinvent definitions. Today, while the SBA offers a wide variety of instructional materials and assistance in getting government contracts, its original mission of helping out *truly* small businesses—entrepreneurs and small, local companies—has been pretty much co-opted by successive administrations (particularly during the Reagan era) and their crony companies.

Now would be a great time to reinvent the SBA from the ground up, making it a place where a person who wants to start an auto repair shop or a small retail store could find the capital to get off the ground. Of course, at the moment that would mean it would be competing with very large and powerful monopolistic banks, so it's a politically unlikely event until the economy *really* crashes hard, taking those banks down with it. Nonetheless, the idea is a good one and should be promoted.

As a nation, we need to get our priorities right when it comes to providing incentives or disincentives for businesses: we need to support small, local businesses, which have created most new jobs historically; we also need to discourage or ban major corporations from their mergers-and-acquisitions mania, close the tax loopholes, and stop the tax subsidies for them. These steps, enforcing the Sherman Antitrust Act, and moving our personal banking to a local credit union—all are good starts toward keeping our towns from getting eaten up by large, predatory corporations.

CHAPTER **4**

An Informed and Educated Electorate

If a nation expects to be ignorant and free, in a state of civilization, it expects what never was and never will be.... Whenever the people are well-informed, they can be trusted with their own government; that, whenever things get so far wrong as to attract their notice, they may be relied on to set them right.

—Thomas Jefferson

TALK RADIO NEWS SERVICE, BASED IN WASHINGTON, D.C., IS owned and run by my dear friend Ellen Ratner. Ellen is an experienced and accomplished journalist, and a large number of interns and young journalism school graduates get their feet wet in reporting by working for and with her.

In March 2010 I was in Washington for a meeting with a group of senators, and I needed a studio from which to do my radio and TV show. Ellen was gracious enough to offer me hers. I arrived as three of her interns were producing a panel-discussion type of TV show for Web distribution at www.talkradionews.com, in which they were discussing for their viewing audience their recent experiences on Capitol Hill.

One intern panelist related that a White House correspondent for one of the Big Three TV networks (ABC, CBS, and NBC) had told her that the network registered a huge amount of interest in the "hot story" that week of a congressman's sexual indiscretions. Far less popular were stories about the debates on health care, the conflicts in the Middle East, and even the Americans who had died recently in Iraq or Afghanistan.

"So that's the story they have to run with on the news," the intern said, relating the substance of the network correspondent's thoughts, "because that's what the American people want to see. If the network doesn't give people what they want to see, viewers will tune away and the network won't have any viewers, ratings, or revenues."

The two other interns commiserated with the first about what a shame it was that Americans wanted the titillating stories instead of the substantive ones, but they accepted without question that the network was therefore *obliged* to "give people what they want."

When they finished their panel discussion, I asked these college students if they knew that there was a time in America when radio and TV stations and networks broadcast the actual news—instead of infotainment—because the law required them to do so. None of them had any idea what I was talking about. They were mystified: why would a station or network broadcast programs that were not popular or not what people wanted?

The Devolution of Broadcast News

But the reality is that from the 1920s, when radio really started to go big in the United States, until Reagan rolled it back in 1987, federal communications law required a certain amount of "public service" programming from radio and television stations as a condition of retaining their broadcast licenses.

The agreement was basic and simple: in exchange for the media owners' being granted a license from the Federal Communications Commission (FCC) to use the airwaves—owned by the public—they had to serve the public interest first, and only then could they go about the business of making money. If they didn't do so, when it came time to renew their license, public groups and individuals could show up at public hearings on the license renewal and argue for the license's being denied.

One small way that stations lived up to their public-service mandate was by airing public-service announcements (PSAs) for local nonprofit groups, community calendars, and other charitable causes. They also had to abide by something called the Fairness Doctrine, which required them to air diverse viewpoints on controversial issues. Separately, during election campaigns, broadcasters had to abide by the Equal Time Rule, which required them to provide equal airtime to rival candidates in an election.

But the biggest way they proved they were providing a public service and meeting the requirements of the Fairness Doctrine was by broadcasting the news. Real news. Actual news. Local, national, and international news produced by professional, old-school journalists.

Because the news didn't draw huge ratings like entertainment shows—although tens of millions of Americans did watch it every night on TV and listened to it at the top of every hour on radio from coast to coast—and because *real* news was expensive to produce, with bureaus and correspondents all over the world, news was a money-loser for all of the Big Three TV networks and for most local radio and TV stations.

But it was such a sacred thing—this was, after all, the keystone that held together the station's license to broadcast and thus to do business—it didn't matter if it lost money. It made all the other money-making things possible.

Through much of the early 1970s, I worked in the newsroom of a radio station in Lansing, Michigan. It had been started and was then run by three local guys: an engineer, a salesman, and a radio broadcaster. They split up the responsibilities like you'd expect, and all were around the building most days and would hang out from time to time with the on-air crew—all except the sales guy. I was forbidden from talking with him because I worked in *news.* There could be no hint—ever, anywhere—that our radio station had violated the FCC's programming-in-the-public-interest mandate by, for example, my going easy on an advertiser in a news story or promoting another advertiser in a different story. News had to be news, separate from profits and revenue—and if it wasn't, I'd be fired on the spot.

News, in other words, wasn't part of the "free market." It was part of our nation's intellectual commons and thus the price of the station's license.

After Reagan blew up the Fairness Doctrine in 1987, two very interesting things happened. The first was the rise of right-wing hate-speech talk radio, starting with Rush Limbaugh that very year. The second, which really stepped up fast after President Clinton signed the Telecommunications Act of 1996, which further deregulated the broadcast industry, was that the money-losing news divisions of the Big Three TV networks were taken under the wings of their entertainment divisions—and wrung dry. Foreign bureaus were closed. Reporters were fired. Stories that promoted the wonders of advertisers or other companies (like movie production houses) owned by the same mega-corporations that owned the networks began to appear. And investigative journalism that cast a bright light on corporate malfeasance vanished.

And because newscasts had ads, and those ads were sold based on viewership, the overall arc and content of the news began to be dictated by what the public *wanted* to know rather than by what they *needed* to know to function in a democratic society.

The interns were aghast. "Reagan did that?!" one said, incredulous. I said yes and that Bill Clinton then helped the process along to its current sorry state by signing the Telecommunications Act, leading to the creation of the Fox "News" Channel in October 1996 and its now-legal ability to call itself a *news* operation while baldly promoting what it knows to be falsehoods or distortions.

Now here we are in 2010, and the news media is an abject failure when it comes to reporting the *real* news—news that citizens in a democracy need to know. Even Ted Koppel, no flaming liberal by any means, said in an April 2010 interview with the British Broadcasting Corporation (BBC) that he thought the state of the news industry was "a disaster."[1] He went on:

> I think we are living through the final stages of what I would call the Age of Entitlement. We fight two wars without raising a single nickel to support them. We feel entitled to mortgages whether we have jobs or not. We feel entitled to make $10 million, $50 million, or $100 million even though the enterprise we headed up is a total failure. And we now feel entitled not to have the news that we *need* but the news that we *want*. We want to listen to news that comes from those who already sympathize with our particular point of view. We don't want the facts anymore.

Koppel was also well aware of the influence of profit-making on the news organizations, which he believed was driving the degradation of news so that it appealed to our baser instincts:

> I think it's the producer [of the particular news show] who is at fault, who desperately needs the consumer...In the good old days, when you only had three networks—ABC, NBC, and CBS—there was competition, but the competition still permitted us to do what was in the public interest. These days all the networks have to fight with the dozens of cable outlets that are out there, the Internet that is out there, and they are all competing for the almighty dollar, and the way to get there is to head down to the lowest common denominator.

When we talk about news that people "need," we are really talking about the intellectual and informational nutrition that is essential for the health and the well-being of our democracy. We need an educated and informed citizenry to participate in our democratic institutions and elections, and we're not going to get that if we keep dumbing down the news and giving people what they want and not what they and society need.

Breaking Up the Media Monopolies

The Studio System

Back in the 1930s and 1940s, the eight biggest movie studios owned the majority of movie theaters in America. A Paramount theater, for example, would show only movies produced by Paramount's movie studios, which featured only people under contract to Paramount. The result was that the studios could make (or break) any movie star and control what people could see in their local community. It was very profitable to the studios, but it was stifling to competition and creativity and therefore a disservice to the moviegoing audience.

So through that era, in a series of actions that lasted almost a decade and which were capped by the big studios' signing a major consent decree with the feds, the federal government tried to force the big theaters to open up the business to competition. The big theaters said that they would, even agreeing to the 1940 Paramount Decree, but they continued with business as usual.

The issue came to a head when it was argued in an antitrust case before the U.S. Supreme Court in 1948. The Court, in a 7-to-1 decision, ruled against the movie giants, saying that they could no longer have total control of the vertically integrated system—from contracting with actors to making movies to showing them in their own theaters across the country. They had to choose: operate in either the movie *making* business or the movie *showing* business. They couldn't do both.

The result was the beginning of the end of the "kingmaker" movie studio monopoly and a boon for independent filmmakers. It also led to a proliferation of new theaters, from ones in urban areas (many retrofitting old opera or burlesque houses) to the new fad of drive-in movie theaters. The industry today is infinitely more diverse and creative as a result of that breakup.

Television and the Prime Time Access Rule

In the late 1960s, television was going through a similar vertical integration, with the Big Three TV networks dominating the content of local television stations they either owned or had as affiliates. In response the FCC promulgated the Prime Time Access Rule in 1970, which dictated that at least one hour out of the four "prime time" hours on every local TV station in the nation would have to come from some source other than the network.

This opened the door to independent TV production companies, like MTM Enterprises, which produced several sitcoms derived from the work of Mary Tyler Moore, and competition from the new television divisions of old-line movie houses, such as Twentieth Century Fox's producing a TV version of *M*A*S*H* and Paramount's producing *Happy Days*.[2]

Although the rules against vertical theater integration are no longer enforced, and the Prime Time Access Rule was blown up in 1996, both the movie and TV industries are broadly more diverse in their programming than they would have been without these "market interventions" that increased competition and decreased monopoly. Which brings us to radio.

The Vicious Circle of Conservative Talk Radio

Many people wonder why the big 50,000-watt AM stations (and even many of the big 25,000- and 10,000-watt stations) across the country carry exclusively conservative programming, particularly programs featuring Rush Limbaugh, Sean Hannity, and Glenn Beck. In most cases, it's a simple matter of the economics of monopoly.

One of the largest owners of the biggest (full-power) radio stations in the country is a mega-corporation that also owns the largest talk-radio syndication service in the nation. When the corporation's stations carry shows that its syndication service owns, it makes money both from the local station ownership and from the ownership of the syndication service. When the stations carry shows from other syndicators or independent shows, the corporation loses the syndication revenue and the local station (which it also owns) loses typically five minutes of advertising inventory per hour that it must barter with the syndicated show for in exchange for the right to air the show.

Thus, so long as the radio industry is allowed to run like the movie studio system in the 1940s, the "studio"—in this case the giant corporation that owns radio stations as well as the nation's largest talk-radio syndication service—will have an outsized influence on what shows up on the very biggest stations in the largest markets across the country. Because of the huge, booming voice of those stations, those shows will have a significant edge in "finding" listeners (and vice versa), making those shows "successful" and thus creating demand for them from the independent stations. It becomes a self-fulfilling prophecy.

Some progressives have suggested that radio needs a "fairness doctrine" where a government panel will determine how much "liberal" or "conservative" programming each station carries and then force the stations to "balance" out any disequilibrium. But who decides what is "liberal" or "conservative"? Is there a checklist of political positions that a government watchdog would have to go through—immigration, taxes, protecting the commons, gay rights, abortion, gun control, foreign policy? It would be a mess, particularly since many of those issues don't lend themselves to easy pigeonholing.

A much easier way to balance the playing field is simply to bring into the marketplace real competition by separating syndication companies from local radio stations so that the stations will no longer have an incentive to carry programming because "it's in the family" and instead will look for shows that can attract and hold an audience.

Programming in the Public Interest

We need to return to the notion of "programming in the public interest," making news back into news. We also need to start enforcing the Sherman Antitrust Act and use it to break up the large media monopolies that have re-formed since the Reagan and Clinton eras, thus effectively rolling back media deregulation.

And this isn't limited to radio and TV. Consumer-friendly regulation almost always has a similar effect in breaking up monopolies when it's designed to help people get around the monopoly.

For example, the company that owns the copper wires, cable, G3 or G4 wireless, or fiber-optic cabling going into your house also owns the exclusive right to carry the content that goes over that infrastructure. If you have a cable company supplying your home, it's probably competing only with the local phone company for your business. Because those two companies (and maybe a mobile provider) are the only ones "competing" for your business, they can easily keep prices—and profits—very high.

In most other developed countries, however, regardless of who owns and maintains the wires, cable, or fiber, *anybody* can offer content over it. The rationale for this is that infrastructure of physical wires and the wireless frequencies constitutes a "natural monopoly" that heavily uses public spaces (cables and phone lines go through and along public streets and rights-of-way); and so while a company can make a small profit on that part of its business, the wires and the wireless frequencies are really a part of the commons that can be regulated.

On the other hand, these developed countries believe that the content *delivery* should be competitive. After all, this is where most of the innovation comes from: it's not a matter of the newest, coolest copper wires; it's the *content* that draws customers.

The result of this is that the average citizen in France, for example, pays about $33 per month for what the *New York Times* described as "Internet service twice as fast as what you get from Verizon or Comcast, bundled with digital high-definition television, unlimited long distance and international calling to 70 countries and wireless Internet connectivity for your laptop or smartphone throughout most of the country."[3]

And that's all from private companies, with no government subsidies. Why? Because small and new companies are *allowed* to compete by the government's *requiring* whichever company carries the signal (wire, cable, fiber, wireless) to make that signal path available to *any* company that wants to offer content to consumers.

Competition—mandated by the French government—has driven the price down and innovation up. The average French citizen is not only paying one-fifth of what the average American pays for such services but is also getting better quality, more variety, and much faster Internet access.

Breaking up the media monopolies and fostering more competition, innovation, and creativity in the media world clearly has public benefits, especially in ensuring that people have access to information they need to participate in our democracy. An informed and educated electorate would be one major result of such government regulation.

The same result can also be helped by making higher education more accessible to the average American.

Access to Higher Education

Jefferson's Tombstone

Thomas Jefferson's tombstone contains an epitaph that he wrote before his death with a directive that not a single word be changed. He had been the president of the United States for two terms and the vice president for one, was a member of the Virginia legislature, and was a famous inventor and architect as well as the author of nearly a million words in various letters, diaries, notebooks,

books, pamphlets, and rants. But he chose not to mention any of that on his gravestone.

Besides the dates of his birth and death, he chose to be remembered for three things that he did in his 83 years of life on earth:

HERE WAS BURIED THOMAS JEFFERSON

AUTHOR OF THE DECLARATION OF AMERICAN INDEPENDENCE

OF THE STATUTE OF VIRGINIA FOR RELIGIOUS FREEDOM

AND FATHER OF THE UNIVERSITY OF VIRGINIA

Writing the Declaration of Independence was an obvious choice, and declaring forever his opposition to integrating church and state also made sense (although it got him demoted in 2010 in schoolbooks in the state of Texas). But "Father of the University of Virginia" being more important than "President of the United States of America"?

Jefferson, it turns out, had this wacky idea. He actually believed that young people should be able to go to college regardless of their ability to pay, their station in life, and how rich or poor their parents were. He thought that an educated populace was the best defense of liberty and democracy in the new nation he'd helped birth.

So the University of Virginia that he started was *free.*

Reagan's Legacy

Ronald Reagan certainly thought that that was a wacky idea, and he was diametrically opposed to the Jeffersonian ideal. When he took office as governor of California in 1967, he quickly called for an end to free tuition at the University of California and an across-the-board 20 percent cut in state funding for higher education.[4] He then argued for a cut in spending on construction for higher education in the state and set up the firing of the popular president of the university, Clark Kerr, whom he deemed "too liberal."

When asked why he was doing away with free college in California, Reagan said that the role of the state "should not be to subsidize intellectual curiosity."

Reagan further referred to college students who nationwide were protesting the Vietnam War as "brats," "cowardly fascists," and "freaks." Adding that if the only way to "restore order" on the nation's campuses was violence, that was fine with him. Just a few days before the Kent State shootings, he famously said, "If it takes a bloodbath, let's get it over with. No more appeasement!"[5]

The trend that Reagan began with the UC system continues to this day. During Republican governor Arnold Schwarzenegger's tenure, state funding for education saw drastic cuts and tuition for undergraduate students rose by more than 90 percent.[6]

Reagan set a tone as governor of California that metastasized across the nation through the 1970s and became federal policy when he was elected president in 1980. By the time he left office in 1988, federal funding for education in the United States had declined from 12 percent of total national educational spending in 1980 to just 6 percent.[7]

Interestingly, to find most of this information you have to dive into recent biographies of the former president or read old newspaper archives that are usually not available online. Not a word of Reagan's role in slashing the UC funding exists, for example, on the Wikipedia pages for either the University of California or Reagan himself. Conservative foundations have poured millions of dollars into campaigns to scrub the Internet clean when it comes to Reagan's past (and that of most other right-wingers).

Yet the reality is that before the Reagan presidency, it was possible for any American student with academic competence to attend college and graduate without debt.

Even in Michigan in the late 1960s, where education was not free but was highly subsidized by the state, my wife paid her way through college by working part-time as a waitress at a Howard

Johnson's. To the extent that I went to college (I completed less than a year altogether), I paid my own way by working as a DJ for $2.35 per hour, running my own TV repair business, pumping gas, and working as a cook at a Big Boy restaurant on weekends.

Such a scenario is unthinkable today. Instead public higher education has become a big business and is often totally corporate; costs are through the roof; and if you're not from a very wealthy family, odds are you'll graduate college with a debt that can take decades to repay. As a result, the United States is slipping in virtually every measurement of innovation, income, and competitiveness. A highly educated workforce is good for innovation and entrepreneurialism: every one of the top 20 innovative countries in the world—except the USA—offers free or very inexpensive college to qualified students.

Ireland took a cue from the pre-Reagan University of California and began offering free college tuition to all Irish citizens and a flat-rate registration fee of 900 euros per year for all European Union citizens. The result, decades later, is that Ireland has gone from having a backwater economy that was largely based on agriculture and tourism to becoming one of the high-tech and innovation capitals of the world.

Ironically, Ireland's vision—and California's pre-Reagan vision—of education was at the core of Thomas Jefferson's hopes for the country he helped found.

Jefferson's Vision

On June 14, 1898, more than 70 years after Jefferson's death, a new building (then called the Academic Building, now called Cabell Hall) was inaugurated at the University of Virginia. One of the nation's most prominent attorneys at the time, James C. Carter of New York City, gave the dedication speech.[8] Carter noted that when Jefferson retired from public office, he was only 66 years old and still energetic and enthusiastic to do something for his country. That something was founding the University of Virginia. Carter said:

> He had cherished through life a passion for the acquisition of knowledge, and was one of the best educated men, if not the best educated man, of his country and time...

> He had in early manhood formed a scheme of public education, which, from time to time, had pressed itself on his attention throughout even the busiest years of his public life. It was part of his political philosophy.

> Lover of liberty as he was, firmly as he believed that popular government was the only form of public authority consistent with the highest happiness of men, he yet did not believe that any nation or community could permanently retain this blessing without the benefit of the lessons of truth, and the discipline of virtue to be derived only from the intellectual and moral education of the whole people.

Carter noted that Jefferson had laid out, in numerous letters and discussions throughout his life, a broad overview of how education should be conducted in the United States. Jefferson envisioned the division of states into districts and wards with primary schools and the establishment of colleges and universities where deserving students "might acquire, *gratis*, a further and higher education."

Jefferson envisioned the goal of free public education—from childhood through university—to be straightforward. In a report he prepared for a state commission in Virginia, Jefferson laid out the six purposes of education:[9]

1. To give to every citizen the information he needs for the transaction of his own business.

2. To enable him to calculate for himself, and to express and preserve his ideas, his contracts and accounts in writing.

3. To improve, by reading, his morals and faculties.

4. To understand his duties to his neighbors and country, and to discharge with competence the functions confided to him by either.

5. To know his rights; to exercise with order and justice those he retains; to choose with discretion the fiduciary of those he delegates; and to notice their conduct with diligence, with candor and judgment.

6. And, in general, to observe with intelligence and faithfulness, all the social relations under which he shall be placed.

In other words, a well-educated citizenry can "choose with discretion" the elected representatives who are the holders of our government that protects our rights, and hold those politicians accountable "with diligence, with candor and judgment."

Ronald Reagan, on the other hand, promised during his election campaign of 1980 to "eliminate the Department of Education" from the federal government; and he appointed his friend William Bennett, who had campaigned and written extensively about destroying the federal Department of Education, as secretary of education—akin to asking the fox to guard the chicken coop. Between Reagan's ax hacking at the roots of our educational systems and his tax cuts to "starve the beast" of government, we are now left with the highest illiteracy rate in the developed world and an electorate that is spectacularly vulnerable to demagoguery and cynical political manipulation.

The experiment of Reaganomics and Reagan's anti-intellectual worldview are demonstrably disordered and dead; we must put them behind us and build anew our country on the solid Jeffersonian foundation of good and free education for all.

Combine that with breaking up the media monopolies in this country and fostering competition and its attendant innovation through intelligent regulation of the "natural monopolies" in our nation, and we would have a more informed citizenry with better and faster access to *real* news and information—including information about our body politic.

These "radical" concepts of free public education all the way up to graduate degrees, breaking up companies that vertically integrate entire markets (particularly in the media), and requiring infrastructure-owning companies to offer their infrastructure to a wide variety of competitors work quite well in dozens of countries around the world. They can here too.

CHAPTER 5

Medicare "Part E"— for Everybody

The Great Society is a place where every child can find knowledge to enrich his mind and to enlarge his talents. It is a place where the city of man serves not only the needs of the body and the demands of commerce but the desire for beauty and the hunger for community. It is a place where men are more concerned with the quality of their goals than the quantity of their goods."

—Lyndon Baines Johnson

THERE ARE TWO IMPORTANT REASONS FOR HAVING A STRONG SO-cial safety net, one based in sound economic policy and the other in our common humanity. So it's no surprise that the countries that have strong social safety nets tend to have resilient economies *and* a higher quality of life.

Ultimately, social safety nets are about managing risk and unforeseen contingencies. On the one hand, there are the risks that we *want* people to take, such as starting a new business. On the other hand, there are unforeseen events that are so severe—like becoming paralyzed in an accident—that no one person (unless incredibly wealthy) could handle the expenses associated with them. In both cases, by setting up a social safety net that distributes the costs of responding to them across the wide spectrum of society, we minimize both the societal cost and the individual suffering.

I've started seven businesses in my life, five of them successful enough that my wife, Louise, and I could sell them off, take about a year of retirement (*better to retire when you're young* was our philosophy), and have enough left over to start the next company. In most cases, when we started the business we had no health insurance, even though in every case we had children.

But we were young and healthy and so were our children (one was a home birth whom I "delivered," although Louise would rightly point out that she did most of the work), and so we did take what, in retrospect, seem like pretty dumb risks: for the initial year or two of setting up a business, we would have no health insurance for ourselves or our employees. We simply couldn't afford it, and so we went without it until the business started earning enough money to pay for it.

Of course, this being the era from the late 1960s to the 1990s, health insurance was heavily regulated by most states, usually offered by nonprofit companies, and relatively inexpensive, so our "stupid" periods weren't usually particularly long or dangerous. But that is no longer the case. Employer-sponsored health insurance costs have skyrocketed in the past decade, far above inflation or workers' wages.

According to a Kaiser Family Foundation report, "between 1999 and 2009, health insurance premiums rose 131 percent, a much faster rate of increase than general inflation (28 percent) or workers' earnings (38 percent)." The report also had this shocking statistic about the amount spent by employers on group health insurance policies: "The amount grew over twenty-fold from $25 billion in 1960 to $545 billion in 2008."[1]

When premiums skyrocket, the usual response from the insurance companies is that they are simply passing along the increase in health-care costs to the consumers. And the corporate media never ask whether the profits of these insurance companies are also suffering. In reality they are making out like bandits, as a 2009 report from Health Care for America Now shows:[2]

> Profits at 10 of the country's largest publicly traded health insurance companies in 2007 rose 428 percent from 2000 to 2007, from $2.4 billion to $12.9 billion, according to U.S. Securities and Exchange Commission filings. In 2007 alone the chief executive officers at these companies collected combined total compensation of $118.6 million—an average of $11.9 million each. That is 468 times more than the...average American worker made that year.

What we have in America today is a trend of higher profits for insurance companies, higher premiums for employers and employees, and an increasing number of small-business owners and entrepreneurs worrying about the health-care costs of doing business.

But in every other developed country (and many that are considered below that threshold, like Costa Rica), entrepreneurs don't have to take such risks. And the result is that the United States is being hammered in the area of innovation by countries that have stronger social safety nets. The *Economist* magazine recently published a study sponsored by Cisco Systems titled "A New Ranking of the World's Most Innovative Countries."[3]

During the period the study was conducted, every country in the top 20, including number 19, Slovenia, had a national health-care system that covered every citizen regardless of employment—except the United States. Japan, Switzerland, and Finland beat us out, and right on our heels were Sweden, Germany, Taiwan, and the Netherlands. The study noted, "The high rank for three small wealthy European states reflects the fact that their economic, social and political conditions favour innovation....The slippage of the U.S. confirms the gradual erosion in recent years of that country's traditional position as the world's technological leader—a trend we expect to continue."

The country that brought the world Thomas Edison and George Westinghouse and Andrew Carnegie has now slid in innovation, in part because of our lack of a strong social safety net.

Praveen Ghanta, a Louisiana resident and a graduate of the Massachusetts Institute of Technology who runs the True Cost blog, notes that of the 33 acknowledged "developed" nations in the world, 32 of them have universal health care for all their citizens. The single exception is the United States. The other 32 countries have some version of universal health care: a single-payer system in which the government pays all bills; a two-tier system, where government provides basic coverage for everyone and nonprofit companies compete to offer high-end services to consumers; or an "insurance mandate" system, where the government requires everyone to have health insurance and insurers are barred from rejecting sick individuals (see sidebar).

Countries with Universal Health Care

The table on the facing page was developed in August 2009 by True Cost, a blog written by Praveen Ghanta. It shows that 32 of the 33 developed nations (those that ranked at 0.9 or higher on a 0-to-1 scale on the United Nations Human Development Index) have universal health care (UHC), with the United States being the lone exception. Note that universal health care does not imply government-only or even government-run health care, as many countries implementing a universal health-care plan continue to have both public and private insurance and medical providers.

Types of Universal Health Care

Single payer The government provides insurance for all residents (or citizens) and pays all health-care expenses except co-pays and co-insurance. Providers may be public, private, or a combination of both.

Two-tier The government provides or mandates catastrophic or minimum insurance coverage for all residents (or citizens)

(continued)

Country	Start date of UHC	Type of UHC
Norway	1912	Single Payer
New Zealand	1938	Two-Tier
Japan	1938	Single Payer
Germany	1941	Insurance Mandate
Belgium	1945	Insurance Mandate
United Kingdom	1948	Single Payer
Kuwait	1950	Single Payer
Sweden	1955	Single Payer
Bahrain	1957	Single Payer
Brunei	1958	Single Payer
Canada	1966	Single Payer
Netherlands	1966	Two-Tier
Austria	1967	Insurance Mandate
United Arab Emirates	1971	Single Payer
Finland	1972	Single Payer
Slovenia	1972	Single Payer
Denmark	1973	Two-Tier
Luxembourg	1973	Insurance Mandate
France	1974	Two-Tier
Australia	1975	Two-Tier
Ireland	1977	Two-Tier
Italy	1978	Single Payer
Portugal	1979	Single Payer
Cyprus	1980	Single Payer
Greece	1983	Insurance Mandate
Spain	1986	Single Payer
South Korea	1988	Insurance Mandate
Iceland	1990	Single Payer
Hong Kong	1993	Two-Tier
Singapore	1993	Two-Tier
Switzerland	1994	Insurance Mandate
Israel	1995	Two-Tier
United States	2014	Insurance Mandate

while allowing the purchase of additional voluntary insurance or fee-for-service care when desired. In Singapore all residents receive a catastrophic policy from the government coupled with a health savings account that they use to pay for routine care. In other countries, such as Ireland and Israel, the government provides a core policy, which the majority of the population supplements with private insurance.

Insurance mandate The government mandates that all citizens purchase insurance, whether from private, public, or nonprofit insurers. In some cases, the insurer list is quite restrictive, while in others a healthy private market for insurance is simply regulated and standardized by the government. In this kind of system, insurers are barred from rejecting sick individuals, and individuals are required to purchase insurance to prevent typical health-care market failures from arising.

Source: Praveen Ghanta, www.truecostblog.com. Reprinted with permission.

As journalist and author T. R. Reid pointed out in his seminal 2008 documentary, *Sick around the World,* and in his subsequent book on the topic, *The Healing of America: A Global Quest for Better, Cheaper, and Fairer Health Care,* the United States is the only industrialized nation in the world that allows for-profit corporations to offer basic, primary-care health insurance. While many countries allow for-profit players in the insurance market, they're specialized; the insurance will get you a single room or suite in a private hospital or covers things like elective cosmetic surgery—basically health insurance add-ons for the rich. But every other nation except the United States considers health care a *right* instead of a *privilege,* so they let only nonprofit companies provide insurance for it, or the nations' governments provide it themselves.[4]

Thus the same inescapable conclusion: America should offer universal health care because it is sound economic policy, because it leads to better innovation in the business sector, and—most importantly—because it ought to be a basic human right in a modern, industrialized democracy.

The Obama Compromise

It took a full year for President Obama and the Democrats to push, pull, and shove through Congress a relatively modest set of changes in the way that health insurance is administered in the United States. The bill that Obama eventually signed on March 22, 2010—titled the Patient Protection and Affordable Care Act—had been sufficiently watered down so that it posed no threat to the profits of the insurance companies and the pharmaceutical companies. The changes were so benign from the point of view of the health insurance industry that its stock prices actually went *up* the day after the legislation was passed. Ditto for the drug giants.

President Obama was so fixed on getting "bipartisan" approval (he did get one Republican senator—Olympia Snowe of Maine—to vote for the bill in committee), that long before any bill came to a vote he embarked on a strategy to buy his own insurance, so to speak, for passage of the bill by addressing the concerns of the health insurance and pharmaceutical companies so that they would not lobby against it on Capitol Hill.

To buy their silence, if not their support, he made a series of major concessions: there would be no "public option" to compete with them to lower premiums (thus protecting insurance company profits and CEO salaries), there would be limits on importing drugs from abroad (thus protecting drug company profits and CEO salaries), and Medicare would be allowed to negotiate drug prices with Big Pharma only on a very limited basis over an extended period of time (more drug company profits). What's more, the insurance mandate would send 30 million new Americans to the industry as customers. No surprise, then, that stock prices rose upon passage of the bill.

Reforming health *insurance* in the United States was probably a bigger job than reforming health *care* would have been. The reason is because the process required building entirely new structures of regulation and management. Such new laws and institutions required a supermajority of 60 of the Senate's 100 senators to overcome a continuous filibuster, something the Republicans began using quite freely since Obama's election.

Ironically, it's much easier to expand an existing program. If legislation is considered in the Senate that only adjusts the amounts of revenue coming in or going out, it can be done through a process called "reconciliation," which requires only a simple majority—50 votes—to pass, with the vice president to break a tie.

For example, George W. Bush and the Republicans used reconciliation—majority rule—to push through his huge cuts in taxes on the richest Americans *three different times* in the first decade of this century. They were not creating a new program but simply adjusting the revenue figures. Ronald Reagan had done the same. If legislation has to do only with revenue or scale adjustments to existing programs, 50 votes in the Senate are enough.

Therein lies the greatest—and the simplest—opportunity to truly reform health care.

We already have Medicare, which is a fairly comprehensive basic health insurance/health-care program that covers nearly all Americans over 65 years of age. It is, in essence, a single-payer health-care program. Obama and the Democrats could easily push to expand the Medicare program to allow Americans of all ages to participate in it, and all they'd need is a simple majority, not a supermajority.

And here's the most amazing part: this would be totally consistent with what President Lyndon B. Johnson and the folks in his administration and Congress had in mind when they created Medicare in July 1965.

The Birth of Medicare

Robert M. Ball was the commissioner of Social Security through the administrations of three presidents—John F. Kennedy, Lyndon B. Johnson, and Richard M. Nixon. He'd worked his way up in the Social Security Administration to become its head guy, spending 30 years of his life there; and then, after he retired, he was tapped by Ronald Reagan to be on the commission that, in 1983, overhauled Social Security to keep it solvent through the Baby Boomer retirement phase.

Medicare was established as an add-on to Social Security, not as a standalone program, so Ball was intimately involved in its creation as commissioner of Social Security throughout the Johnson years. He sat in on the meetings with members of the House and the Senate, he was involved in the writing of the Medicare legislation, and he was the man charged with helping implement it after LBJ signed it into law on July 30, 1965. He even ceremonially presented the first Medicare cards to Harry and Bess Truman.

Given his catbird seat during this entire process, Ball felt it important to put his recollections into the historical record, which he did in a 1995 article for *Health Affairs* journal titled "Perspectives on Medicare." "Because I was deeply involved in the development, enactment, and implementation of the [Medicare] program," he wrote, "my recollections may be of use in rounding out the historical record." His article was appropriately subtitled "What Medicare's Architects Had in Mind."[5]

Perhaps the most important thing the drafters had in mind, Ball wrote, was that Medicare was the first step in a more far-reaching solution to America's health-care problem:

> For persons who are trying to understand what we were up to, the first broad point to keep in mind is that all of us who developed Medicare and fought for it—including Nelson Cruikshank and Lisbeth Schorr of the AFL-CIO and Wilbur Cohen, Alvin David, Bill Fullerton, Art Hess, Ida Merriam, Irv Wolkstein,

myself, and others at the Social Security Administration—had been advocates for universal national health insurance. We saw insurance for the elderly as a fallback position, which we advocated solely because it seemed to have the best chance politically. Although the public record contains some explicit denials, we expected Medicare to be a first step toward universal national health insurance, perhaps with "Kiddicare" as another step.

In his article Ball talks about how national health insurance had actually once been advocated by the American Medical Association (AMA), whose leaders "were favorably impressed by the systems that had been established in Germany (1883) and Britain (1911), and several other countries around that time." This was 1916, he notes, and "ironically, much of the American labor movement in 1916 was opposed" to national health insurance, as "Samuel Gompers, president of the American Federation of Labor (AFL), preferred collective bargaining to political solutions and feared that if workers began leaning on government, they might begin to look generally in that direction, rather than to unions, for help."

A decade later, Ball notes, the AMA and AFL positions had reversed and stayed that way up to and through the development of Medicare. The AMA was so vehemently opposed to government-offered health insurance that it even hired Hollywood actor and tobacco industry spokesman Ronald Reagan to produce an LP record titled *Ronald Reagan Speaks Out against Socialized Medicine*, which would be played at coffee klatches held by doctors' wives nationwide to generate letters to Congress against the Medicare plan.

"The AMA's opposition approached hysteria," Ball wrote, noting that during the Truman administration the advocacy of the president for a national single-payer system so frightened the AMA that "members were assessed dues for the first time to create a $3.5 million war chest—very big money for the times—with which the association conducted an unparalleled campaign of vituperation against the advocates of national health insurance." This was, he notes, "a warm-up for the later campaign against Medicare."

So how did Medicare get passed?

Ball lays it out quite simply: old people were not profitable for the health insurance companies, so they were happy to get them off their rolls and onto the government's. "[The elderly] used, on average, more than twice as many hospital days as younger persons used but had, on average, only about half as much income. Private insurers, who set premiums to cover current costs, had to charge the elderly much more, and the elderly could not afford the charges."

This set the stage for Medicare, and the health insurance companies were at first enthusiastic about it. But in the final days of the development of the Medicare program, word got out that the people putting it together, including President Johnson, saw it as a system that could easily be modified to cover all Americans by the simple process of lowering the eligibility age, presumably incrementally over a decade or two. This pushed the insurance companies over the edge, prompting on their part a "fervent desire to keep government from penetrating further into the insurance business." Ball adds, "Although most business groups opposed Medicare, the insurance industry was the AMA's main ally [in that opposition]."

But because people knew and trusted Social Security, and this was just a health-benefit add-on to that existing program, it was easy to sell in Congress and to the American people. It was one of the most important legislative accomplishments of the Johnson administration.

It's been more than 45 years since Medicare was legislated into existence, and it was established with the idea that one day it would be slightly tweaked to become *the* national single-payer health insurance program for the United States of America.

Medicare for All

So here we are, with a long-standing and successful Medicare program that everyone understands. Medicare has four parts: Part A covers hospital stays, Part B pays for medical services, Part C pays for private insurance coverage, and Part D covers prescription drugs.

It's time now to create "Medicare Part E," which covers "everybody." Just let any citizen in the United States buy into Medicare.

It would be so easy. There is no need to reinvent the wheel with the so-called "public option," which would mean setting up a whole new program from the ground up. Medicare already exists. It works. Some people will like it; others won't, just like the Post Office versus FedEx analogy that President Obama has used so often.

Just pass a simple bill—it could probably be just a few lines, like when Medicare was expanded to include disabled people— that says that *any* American citizen can buy into the program at a rate to be set by the Centers for Medicare and Medicaid Services (CMS) and the Department of Health and Human Services that reflects the actual cost for us to buy into it.

Thus, Medicare Part E would be revenue neutral!

And as we saw earlier, if you are not creating a new program, with its own set of rules and regulations and management system, but only making changes to an existing program, you can get it through Congress with a simple majority and never face the threat of a filibuster or having to water things down to get enough votes for a supermajority.

To make it available to people with a low income, Congress could raise the rates slightly for all currently noneligible people to cover the cost of subsidizing families that live below 200 percent of the federal poverty level. Revenue neutral again.

This would blow up all the rumors about "death panels" and "pulling the plug on Grandma" and everything else: everybody knows what Medicare is. And nobody would be forced to enroll in Medicare. Those who scorn it and think of it as "socialized medicine" can give their hard-earned pay to United Healthcare so that it can pay its CEO $744 million in stock options. Those who like Medicare can buy into Part E. Simplicity itself.

Of course, we'd like a few fixes, like letting Medicare negotiate with pharmaceutical companies to get volume discounts on drug prices, and filling some of the other holes Republicans and AARP and lobbyists for Big Insurance have drilled into Medicare that now pretty much require people to buy "supplemental" for-profit insurance, but that can wait for the second round. Let's get this done first.

And if this fails—if Congress can't get out from under its corporate overlords—there is another solution embedded in the Obama legislation that passed in March 2010. Senator Ron Wyden of Oregon put into the health-care bill an amendment—which passed and is now law—titled "Empowering States to Be Innovative" that lets any state apply to the secretary of Health, Education, and Welfare (HEW) for a waiver from the national health insurance mandate program. The secretary has 180 days to deny the waiver with cause (Wyden can't imagine what the cause may be other than perhaps there being a Republican in the White House appointing the HEW secretary). After that the state can start its own single-payer health-care system—with or without an insurance mandate, with or without a public option—so long as the state system meets or exceeds the coverage requirements of the federal legislation.

So far California's legislature has twice passed a law to set up a statewide single-payer health insurance system, and Vermont did just weeks before this writing, in April 2010. In California's case, Republican Governor Schwarzenegger twice vetoed the legislation, and the Vermont bill has not yet been reviewed by that state's Republican governor for a signature or veto. But eventually some state will successfully pull this off.

This is how Canada moved into the modern health-care era, starting the same year that the United States was helping Germany and Japan write constitutions that declared health care to be a right rather than a privilege (although the Truman administration couldn't get similar legislation through Congress when they submitted a single-payer plan in 1947).

In 1946 the province of Saskatchewan passed the Saskatchewan Hospitalization Act, which was a single-payer system for all citizens of the province covering all medical expenses that required hospitalization. Four years later the province of Alberta followed suit with a somewhat expanded program, creating a single-payer system called Medical Services (Alberta) Incorporated. In 1957 the Canadian federal government got into the act, and by 1961 all 10 provinces of Canada had joined in.

In the United States, Hawaii and Massachusetts have experimented with universal health care, although both had to do it during a time when federal laws made it difficult to impossible to start a true single-payer system, so in both cases the systems rely on the for-profit companies to administer the programs. Although the 2010 law didn't do away with the for-profit health insurance companies' antitrust exemption, it did, according to Senator Wyden, make it explicitly possible for any state to start its own single-payer system that, for the first time, *excludes* the for-profit leeches...er...companies.

Now we can all get active and mobilize to get our own states to set up single-payer systems that are far more inclusive and progressive than the watered-down federal legislation that became law in 2010.

Rebuild the Social Safety Net

If we address the health-care conundrum in America with a single-payer system that is fair and equitable, we will be patching a big hole in our social safety net. The importance of such a change is clear when we compare its impact on innovation and entrepreneurialism across the country with that of other nations that have already done this.

The Reagan experiment of suspending enforcement of the Sherman Antitrust Act wiped out small businesses across the land; college has become prohibitively expensive; health-care costs are out of sight; and our bankruptcy laws were rewritten by the banksters during the Bush Jr. administration to make it harder for entrepreneurs to declare bankruptcy and start over (as Henry Ford, P. T. Barnum, Milton Hershey, and J. H. Heinz all famously did and then bounced back to create successful companies).

The result is what Barry C. Lynn refers to as "the new monopoly capitalism" in America, a process that has turned this country from an entrepreneur's dream into a neo-feudal state where almost all businesses are owned or controlled by a small handful of huge corporations, workers tremble at the specter of unemployment, and the middle class is being wiped out.

It's ironic that the Tea Party populists, most of whom believe that they are furthering the American ideal of "rugged individualism," are supporting mega-corporate-friendly policies like Reaganomics and Clintonomics and are making it very difficult for individuals to be anything other than drones in a giant corporate-run economic machine. And, on the flipside, those countries that call themselves "democratic socialist" in their organization—Finland, Germany, Japan, the Netherlands, Sweden—actually provide a deep and fertile soil into which entrepreneurs may plant new businesses.

Bankruptcy laws that protect innovators and risk-takers are good for entrepreneurialism: all those countries except the United States make it relatively easy to start over.

Not having to put yourself and your family's health at risk to start a business is good for entrepreneurialism: all but the USA offer national health care that is *not* tied to your employer in such a way that you lose health insurance when you quit your job or your first attempt at a new business doesn't succeed.

A strong social safety net is the most powerful way we can encourage innovation and entrepreneurialism. While ideologues will rant about the "dangers" of "big government," the reality is that when government provides this sort of backstop, *individuals* like me—and a whole new generation of entrepreneurs—will step forward to innovate, build, and succeed.

CHAPTER **6**

Make Members of Congress Wear NASCAR Patches

The liberty of a democracy is not safe if the people tolerate the growth of private power to a point where it comes stronger than their democratic state itself. That, in its essence, is fascism—ownership of government by an individual, by a group.

—Franklin D. Roosevelt

STARTED MY FIRST BUSINESS AT THE AGE OF 17 WITH $25. I PAID that amount to rent a shelf in a head shop (which sold mostly pipes, bongs, and cigarette papers) across the street from Michigan State University in East Lansing. The shelf had a sign: "The Electronics Joint—leave your stereo or TV here for repair, and we'll return it fixed within a week. Free estimate of charges before work is done." The guy who ran the head shop managed the shelf for 10 percent of our revenues plus the $25-per-month shelf rental; within two years the venture had grown to include five employees, and we moved into our own storefront down the street.

As the business grew, however, I didn't manage it wisely and ended up about $3,000 in debt, which was a lot of money in 1968 for a part-time student and part-time DJ. Ultimately, I had to shut the company down and go to work full-time as a radio DJ.

That didn't turn out so well either. I got fired when I played two black female artists back-to-back, a violation of station policy at the time, and then refused to promise to never do it again. With my unemployment check, I bought some herbs at a local General Nutrition Center store and started an herbal tea company—Woodley Herber—that grew over the next six years to having 19 employees. One of our products that contained ginseng (which was then hot as an aphrodisiac) was picked up by Larry Flynt to market through his brand-new magazine, *Hustler,* making him a million bucks and turning a nice profit for my partner and me. Louise and I sold our half of that company to our employees in 1978 to move to New Hampshire and start a community for abused kids.

We wiped out our savings buying land for the children's village and living for almost five years on a salary of $25 per week.* I still had an American Express Platinum Card, a leftover from the prosperous Woodley Herber days, so in 1983, with a $10,000 (or was it $15,000?) line of credit and some income from writing for a few magazines (I was contributing editor to seven of them that year), Louise and I moved to Atlanta and opened International Wholesale Travel and its retail operation Sprayberry Travel. That turned out to be quite a success. Within three years we'd marketed the company to the front page of the *Wall Street Journal* and had about $6 million in annual revenues, so we sold the company in 1986 to retire to Germany for a year to do volunteer work for the international relief agency Salem International.

We moved back to Atlanta in 1987 and used about $50,000 we had left from selling the travel company to start an advertising agency, The Newsletter Factory, which quickly grew to generating several million dollars a year in revenue and had about 20 employees. We sold that business to our employees on a seven-year

---

*Although we moved on, the Salem Children's Village is still there and doing fine 30-plus years later; www.salemchildrensvillage.org—it's a great charity if you're inclined to help out!

buyout in 1996 and retired to the backwoods of Vermont to write books and enjoy life.

All of this is a way of saying that I am a somewhat typical "serial entrepreneur," and fortunately we have a lot of them in America. They are generally middle-class people (my dad worked in a tool-and-die shop for 40 years, and my mom was a full-time homemaker with four sons), they generally do not have an inheritance or family money to draw on, and yet they spend their lives pursuing the American Dream.

I have never relied on a member of Congress or a government agency to do me a favor or bend the rules. I have never given campaign contributions to politicians in hopes of getting favors that would help my business. I have never hired a lobbyist to try to amend laws that would serve my financial interest. And this is generally true of *all* the hundreds of thousands of sole proprietors and partnerships and small businesses across America.

But that is *not* how big-time corporate America operates. To them making large campaign contributions and spending millions of dollars each year on lobbyists is just another investment that pays off handsomely. Their motto (in behavior, if not in fact) is *You've got to pay to play.*

This flood of corporate money and influence in our government makes for a decidedly uneven playing field for businesses as well as taints and corrupts our government. Unfortunately, the trend is moving in the direction of allowing even more money to encroach into our politics, thanks to the Supreme Court. The absolutely necessary solution here is to bring honesty and transparency to our politics.

"Capital" Hill

Tom DeLay famously (and apparently illegally—as of this writing he's managed to keep postponing his trial for years) took all sorts of goodies from lobbyists when he was a Republican leader in the

House of Representatives, ranging from campaign contributions to a golf trip to St. Andrews in Scotland, the (incredibly expensive) "home" of the sport. His major patron was Jack Abramoff, lobbyist, businessman, head of conservative organizations—and criminal, sentenced to prison for felonies related to defrauding Indian tribes and plying politicians with gifts in exchange for political favors.

DeLay even went beyond just taking money and favors from lobbyists. He famously told lobbying firms on K Street in Washington, D.C., that they shouldn't even bother to show up at his office looking for favors if they had *any* Democrats working in their offices. In 2005, DeLay was charged with violations of campaign finance laws and money laundering, while two of his former aides were convicted in the Abramoff scandal.

Similarly, former Republican senator Phil Gramm took a few million dollars over the years (and his wife, on Enron's board of directors, took somewhere between $900,000 and $2 million) from the financial services and energy industries. And then, while still a senator, he slipped into the must-pass 2000 omnibus spending bill a sweet little feature, the 262-page Commodity Futures Modernization Act of 2000 (CFMA), which came to be known as the "Enron loophole."

The CFMA allowed Enron to squeeze an estimated $40 *billion* out of California consumers, creating an energy crisis in the state in 2000 and 2001 and a political crisis for Governor Gray Davis that led to his replacement in 2003 by Republican Arnold Schwarzenegger (nominated for the job after he had a private and largely secret meeting with Enron CEO Ken Lay). It also opened the doors for Wall Street to use the new law to "create" what they called "new financial instruments" like credit default swaps, leading directly to the near-worldwide crash of the banking system in 2008.

After leaving Congress, Gramm followed in the footsteps of more than 100 of his colleagues in the past three decades and became a lobbyist himself in 2002, immediately going to work for UBS, a massive Swiss bank that is the world's second-largest manager of "wealth assets." In 2009, UBS was accused of helping American millionaires and billionaires evade taxes. The IRS filed a lawsuit in February 2009 alleging that 52,000 Americans secretly held up to $14.8 billion in accounts at UBS to avoid paying U.S. income taxes.[1]

As the cases of DeLay and Gramm show (and there are hundreds of similar congressional examples), for major corporations and very rich individuals and families, national or international, campaign contributions and lobbying do produce healthy returns. Invest a few million, make a few billion. Putting money into the careers of members of Congress, past or present, it turns out, is among the most consistently lucrative investments in the world.

As I noted in my book *Unequal Protection,* as of 2009 there were roughly 64 registered lobbyists for every member of Congress—more than 34,750 in total—and 138 of them are former members of Congress. Include state lobbyists, and there are more than 60,000 (because of variations in state laws on what is or isn't a lobbyist, and who and how they should register, this may well be a significant underestimate: nobody really knows the true number).[2]

Senator Bernie Sanders noted on my radio show during the Senate debates on financial services industry regulation that the banking industry was spending more than $1 million per day on lobbying and had hired more than 250 former members of Congress to lobby their peers, including people who had previously been considered to have highly ethical and spotless reputations like former Democratic presidential candidate Dick Gephardt.

As Jeffrey H. Birnbaum noted in the *Washington Post* in June 2005, "The number of registered lobbyists in Washington has more than doubled since 2000 to more than 34,750 while the amount that lobbyists charge their new clients has increased by as much as 100 percent. Only a few other businesses have enjoyed greater prosperity in an otherwise fitful economy." He added that "lobbying firms can't hire people fast enough" and that salaries *started* at $300,000 per year. "Big bucks lobbying is luring nearly half of all lawmakers who return to the private sector when they leave Congress," Birnbaum noted, citing a study by Public Citizen's Congress Watch.[3] The situation has only gotten worse since then.

From Lobbying to Regulating—Another Way Corporations Control Government

One of the primary goals of lobbyists is to affect legislation—introduce new bills or amendments, slip in key provisions, kill bills, and so on. But just as important is to affect regulations being considered by myriad federal agencies that could have huge financial impacts on the lobbyists' corporate clients. So when the lobbyists have friends in the White House, as they did with George W. Bush and Dick Cheney, they actually get to take over the regulatory agencies through appointments.

A Rogues' Gallery

During the Bush Jr. administration, more than a hundred very well paid lobbyists decided to forsake their big incomes for relatively paltry civil service paychecks for a year or two to become the actual regulators of the agencies they used to lobby.

J. Steven Griles, for example, moved from a $585,000-per-year paycheck as a lobbyist for oil and gas interests to become the number two person in the Department of the Interior, right under Interior Secretary Gale Norton, accepting a salary of $150,000 (a pay cut of $435,000 per year). His department then opened 8 million acres of western lands for oil and gas exploration and gave $2 million in no-bid contracts to one of Griles's former clients—while Griles continued to receive a four-year $284,000-per-year bonus from his former employer.[4]

Griles was also helping Jack Abramoff at the Interior Department (a government prosecutor said Griles was "Abramoff's guy at the Interior"); he eventually pleaded guilty to lying to the Senate about his relationship with Abramoff and was sentenced to 10 months in prison and a $30,000 fine.[5]

The *Denver Post* in 2004 looked into the revolving-door phenomenon in the Bush administration, tallying more than 100 "high-level officials under Bush who helped govern industries they once represented as lobbyists, lawyers or company advocates." The newspaper reported:[6]

> In at least 20 cases, those former industry advocates have helped their agencies write, shape or push for policy shifts that benefit their former industries. They knew which changes to make because they had pushed for them as industry advocates. The president's political appointees are making or overseeing profound changes affecting drug laws, food policies, land use, clean-air regulations and other key issues.
>
> Government watchdogs call it a disturbing trend, not adequately restrained by existing ethics laws.

Among the cases the article identified were Charles Lambert, a 15-year lobbyist for the meat industry in its effort to block labeling and mad cow disease investigations, who went to work for the U.S. Department of Agriculture (USDA), where he officially determined that mad cow disease wasn't a threat and shouldn't be investigated and that meat shouldn't be labeled with regard to its safety.

Then there was Daniel E. Troy, a lawyer who worked for a lobbying firm representing Pfizer Inc., Eli Lilly & Co., and others in Big Pharma. In 2001 he left the lobbying firm and became the chief counsel for the Food and Drug Administration (FDA). Mysteriously, the main focus of the FDA's position on regulating the drug companies moved "to discourage frivolous lawsuits, which drive up costs," making it harder for consumers damaged by prescription drug side effects to sue Troy's former employers.

The *Denver Post* story also pointed out the case of Thomas A. Scully, a lobbyist who represented HCA, a huge hospital corporation originally started by Bill Frist's family. HCA was embroiled in a fraud investigation by the federal Centers for Medicare and Medicaid Services, started by a whistleblower. In 2001 Scully left his job to head the CMS. By coincidence, eight months later, the agency worked out a $250 million settlement—which critics said was far too lenient—that kept the feds from looking further into HCA's books and kept the Justice Department away. Under pressure from some members of Congress, the settlement was delayed and eventually HCA ended up paying the $250 million plus $631 million in civil penalties. Scully then left the Centers for Medicare and Medicaid Services and went back to work again as a lobbyist for Medicare providers.

Then there was the case of lobbyist Jeffrey Holmstead, who worked at a law firm that represented big utility companies and which had proposed 12 paragraphs of changes in Environmental Protection Agency (EPA) regulations affecting those utilities. Holmstead then went to work for the EPA as a regulator overseeing the air pollution division, and soon thereafter those 12 paragraphs—which would have given a pollution exemption to 168 of 232 western-based power plants—appeared in proposed EPA rules changes. The case was so blatant that 45 U.S. senators—including three Republicans—and 10 states' attorneys general wrote a letter asking the EPA to void the proposed rule because of "undue industry influence." Their complaints were largely ignored by the Bush administration.

Lobbying as Big Business

Given how lucrative lobbying is as an investment, it's become a huge business. In February 2010 the Center for Responsive Politics laid out which industries had invested how much in Congress the previous year. Overall it found that in 2009 the number of registered lobbyists who actively lobbied Congress was 13,694 and the total lobbying spending was a whopping $3.47 *billion*—a 240 percent increase since 1999.

The report showed that the top federal lobbying spending was carried out in 2009 by the health-care sector ($543.9 million); followed by the finance, insurance, and real estate sector ($465 million); and energy and natural resources ($408.9 million) (see Table 1 below). Among the biggest lobbying clients were the U.S. Chamber of Commerce ($144.5 million), ExxonMobil

Table 1   Top Congressional Lobbying Spending in 2009 by Sector

Sector	Total (in dollars)
Miscellaneous business (retail, manufacturing, etc.)	558,230,086
Health	543,992,861
Finance, insurance and real estate	465,018,131
Energy and natural resources	408,966,962
Communications/electronics	360,048,798
Other (education, nonprofits, religious)	247,684,383
Transportation	243,941,558
Ideological/single-issue	153,357,071
Agribusiness	141,834,541
Defense	135,879,762
Construction	56,759,414
Labor	43,391,295
Lawyers and lobbyists	35,020,209

Source: The Center for Responsive Politics
http://www.opensecrets.org/news/2010/02/federal-lobbying-soars-in-2009.html

($27 million), and the pharmaceutical industry group PhRMA ($26 million) (see Table 2 below).

The most recent example of the toxic and pernicious influence of industry in government (as of this writing) is the BP/Transocean/Halliburton oil spill in the Gulf of Mexico. Both

Table 2 Top Congressional Lobbying Spending in 2009 by Client

Lobbying Client	Total (in dollars)
U.S. Chamber of Commerce	144,496,000
ExxonMobil	27,430,000
Pharmaceutical Research & Mfrs. of America	26,150,520
General Electric	25,520,000
Pfizer Inc.	24,619,268
Blue Cross/Blue Shield	22,715,439
AARP	21,010,000
American Medical Association	20,830,000
Chevron Corp.	20,815,000
National Association of Realtors	19,477,000
American Beverage Association	18,850,000
American Hospital Association	18,347,176
ConocoPhillips	18,069,858
Verizon Communications	17,820,000
FedEx Corp.	17,050,000
Boeing Co.	16,850,000
BP	15,990,000
National Cable and Telecommunications Assoc.	15,980,000
Northrop Grumman	15,180,000
AT&T Inc.	14,729,673

Source: The Center for Responsive Politics
http://www.opensecrets.org/news/2010/02/federal-lobbying-soars-in-2009.html

Norway and Brazil allow companies to engage in deep-water offshore drilling, but both of those countries also require by law that companies put blowout preventer devices on all oil wells that can be remotely activated in the event of a catastrophic failure. When Dick Cheney's Energy Task Force (comprising Cheney, a few hand-picked bureaucrats, and executives from the fossil fuels industry, meeting in secret behind closed doors) reviewed a suggestion that the United States put into our regulations a similar provision, they dismissed it as "too expensive." The cost for one of those devices—which would have prevented the BP Gulf spill—is a paltry $500,000 per well.

Rein in Corporate Control of Government

It wasn't always this way. Consider this old Wisconsin statute, broadly representative of laws virtually every state had up until the rise of the robber barons—railroad magnates and other businessmen who became wealthy using anti-competitive and unfair business practices—in the 1880s:[7]

> **Political contributions by corporations.** No corporation doing business in this state shall pay or contribute, or offer consent or agree to pay or contribute, directly or indirectly, *any* money, property, free service of its officers or employees or thing of value to *any* political party, organization, committee or individual for *any* political purpose whatsoever, or for the purpose of influencing legislation of *any* kind, or to promote or defeat the candidacy of *any* person for nomination, appointment or election to *any* political office. [Italics added for emphasis—it makes a great "out loud" read when you shout the word "any".]

The penalty for an individual (representing a corporation) violating such a law was not just a fine but a prison term; and if the corporation itself was found to be violating the law, the penalty could even include the corporate death penalty: *dissolution* of the corporation.

Reflected in that law (and in similar laws across the nation at the time) is a healthy skepticism of corporate interests and motives and an assumption that those interests are often contrary to the larger public interest.

We've gone the wrong way since then.

What we have lost is the moral and ethical view of our civic life and replaced it with a story that says that anything is acceptable so long as it is *legally* permitted. Campaign contributions, lobbyist wining-and-dining, and revolving-door careers—all are seen as legally permissible and that's that, end of story, even though these unethical and immoral acts interfere with our fundamental democratic process and are therefore really crimes against the public good.

The British Lobbying Sting

While lobbying isn't explicitly illegal in the United Kingdom, it's seriously frowned upon, particularly when done by former members of the government. In March 2010 the *Sunday Times* and Britain's privately owned Channel 4 TV ran a sting operation on former cabinet ministers and members of Parliament by pretending to be a U.S. lobbying firm. The reporters-lobbyists approached 20 former members of Parliament (MPs) altogether, 13 from the Labour Party and seven Conservatives, and used hidden cameras to record the conversations. The offer was for the former MPs to try to influence their associates and to do so for 3,000 to 5,000 British pounds per day in payment as lobbyists.[8]

Two out of 20 agreed to do so. No money was paid, no work was done, but the politicians simply agreed to work as lobbyists and use their connections to advance the interests of the (fake) American firm.

When the story hit the newspaper and the hidden camera clips were aired, all hell broke loose. The scandal rocked London. "Ex-ministers in 'Cash for Influence' Row under Fire" screamed the headline on the BBC's Web site, noting that other ministers "have condemned ex-cabinet colleagues who were secretly filmed apparently offering to try to influence government policy in return for cash."

The day after the story hit, the Labour Party suspended three of the cabinet ministers involved in the investigation. The *Guardian* newspaper reported:[9]

> Three former cabinet ministers, Geoff Hoon, Stephen Byers and Patricia Hewitt were suspended from the Parliamentary Labour party last night in an unprecedented crack down on sleaze.
>
> The move was implemented by the party's chief whip, Nick Brown, and fuelled by backbench revulsion at claims that the trio had been using their ministerial experience to seek profitable lobbying consultancies.

What's important to note is the absolute shock expressed by everyone at the basic idea—something we take for granted in America—that politicians would even consider using their connections to make money as lobbyists. The BBC noted in its article that this behavior shocked and horrified even the most senior financial officer in the prime minister's cabinet. Alistair Darling, the chancellor of the Exchequer (similar to Treasury secretary in the United States), told the BBC:[10]

> The best answer when you get a call like that is to put the receiver back down again. It's obvious....But really, what on earth did they think they were doing?
>
> And equally for a company, you don't need a lobbyist. If you've got something to say, go directly to the government department and make your case. It's just ridiculous.

Corporate Bedfellows

So how is it that lobbying is widespread in the developing world (where it's often referred to as "bribery") but rare in developed countries—except for the United States? The answer has much to do with the U.S. Supreme Court's interpretation of the "rights" of corporations and its interpretation of our First Amendment, which forbids the government from limiting "free speech," particularly interpreted to mean *political* free speech.

Supreme Court rulings notwithstanding (more on this in chapter 10), this is definitely not what the Founders of this nation or the Framers of the Constitution had in mind. Numerous legislative solutions to corporations' corrupting politicians with money or influence have been offered over the years, from the Tillman Act of 1907 to the Bipartisan Campaign Reform Act of 2002, commonly known as McCain-Feingold. All have been weakened or even struck down, in whole or in part, by the Supreme Court in its defense of the free-speech rights of very wealthy individuals and corporations.

The most powerful lever that lobbyists have is the campaign contribution, since it costs a member of Congress more than $1 million every two years to get reelected and a senator around $6 million (and far more in the very large states).

So for years now, reform efforts have focused on transparency and limits on campaign contributions and on pushing a system of publicly financing elections to take money out of politics. But all of that has been negated by the Supreme Court, and its latest ruling pretty much puts a nail in the coffin of public financing of campaigns. In 2010 in the *Citizens United v. Federal Election Commission* case, the Supreme Court ruled that corporations—even *foreign* corporations—and wealthy individuals can spend *unlimited* amounts of money to influence elections; they just have to spend it independently of the candidate's or party's official campaign.

So now if a candidate wants a few million dollars spent for his campaign, all he has to do is get the commitment (informally, of course) from a corporation that it'll do it. Assuming the corporation keeps its word, this blows up pretty much every strategy anybody has come up with so far to clean up the elections mess in the United States and will probably lead, over the next few years, to an entirely corporate-controlled and beholden Congress.

Because the Supreme Court (with corporate lawyers like Antonin Scalia and former Monsanto attorney Clarence Thomas, with Thomas's wife working at the corporate- and rich-guy-funded think tank Heritage Foundation) has completely jumped into bed with corporations with the *Citizens United* ruling, about the only real solutions to this are either amending the Constitution or changing the composition of the Court (through attrition over time in the hopes of a Democrat in the White House or through impeachment, which is extremely unlikely). We'll get back to this in detail in chapter 10.

Fix Our Monetary System

But there are other things that we can fix, starting with how we handle our money. Some of this will be helped by having an honest White House and Congress, but other things we can do ourselves right now.

One of the biggest private sectors funneling money into politics these past few years—and causing the revolving door to rotate ever faster—is the financial services industry. As a joint report in late 2009 showed:[11]

> Since the beginning of 2009, organizations in the financial services sector—including banks, investment firms, insurance companies and real estate companies—have commissioned 940 former federal employees as federal lobbyists, Public Citizen's analysis of data provided by the Center for Responsive Politics shows....

> So far in 2009, the industry has employed at least 70 former members of Congress, nearly half of the 150 former members who have reported lobbying in 2009. These include former

Speaker of the House Dennis Hastert (R-Ill.); former Senate
Majority Leader and Republican presidential nominee Bob Dole
(R-Kansas); former Senate Majority Leader Trent Lott (R-Miss.);
former House Majority Leaders Dick Armey (R-Texas) and
Dick Gephardt (D-Mo.); former Appropriations Chairman Bob
Livingston (R-La.); and former Ways & Means Chairman Bill
Thomas (R-Calif.). Former Rep. Vin Weber (R-Minn.) boasts
the most financial sector clients (11) among former members
of Congress.

It is no surprise that financial services corporations are extremely interested in influencing government these days. The financial systems of the United States have been as badly corrupted
by corporate influence as have most of our politicians.

The Fickle Fed

Perhaps the most important player in our national economy is
the Federal Reserve. In reality, the "Fed" is not federal and has
no reserves. The Constitution specifies that only the Treasury
Department—part of the federal government—has the power to
"coin money, [and] regulate the value thereof" and lays out no
provision for a separate corporation such as the Fed to produce
our money supply.

The Fed was created in 1913 by an act of Congress but is a sep-
arate-from-government corporation, owned by its member banks,
which are themselves owned by their stockholders. It therefore,
arguably, has no constitutional authority to "coin money" for us.
To get around the constitutional provision that only the government can mint money, the U.S. Treasury Department still runs
the U.S. mints, where our actual *coins* are produced. If you have
dollar coins, or half-dollars, quarters, dimes, nickels, or pennies,
you have actual money produced by the U.S. government. But if
you have paper money that says "Federal Reserve Note" at the top,
it is not produced by the U.S. government but by the corporate-
bank-owned Federal Reserve.

The distinction is at once significant and irrelevant in this age of electronic money flying across the Internet.

It's significant because in all the years since it was created, the Fed has never been audited. When in 2009 and 2010 Congress wanted to know why the Fed was creating trillions of U.S. dollars electronically out of thin air and "loaning" them to foreign central banks (and wanted to know which banks got them), the Fed bluntly told Congress that it wasn't going to disclose the information. It similarly told members of Congress to take a leap when they asked what banks got Fed help during the Bush Great Crash of 2008. If the Treasury Department controlled our money supply instead, decisions would be more transparent (and subject to Freedom of Information Act lawsuits) and "profits" from handling the money supply would inure to We the People.

It's arguably irrelevant because dollars—even those "created" by the Fed—are backed by the full faith and credit of the United States. We're stuck with them.

There are two "solutions" that people knowledgeable about these matters suggest and that seem to make a lot of sense.

The first solution is that the Federal Reserve be nationalized and brought under the purview of the Treasury Department, so the United States goes back to producing and controlling its own money and money supply. "Banking profits" from the Fed could even help support the federal budget.

In this scenario the Fed would simply be purchased—or taken with compensation under provisions of the Fifth Amendment— by the U.S. government from the private banks that own it.

As we work on that change, we can start with the idea of immediately setting up a system to audit the Fed. We have the system in place to conduct such an audit—the Government Accountability Office (GAO), which audits most other federal agencies. Congress could simply require that the GAO audit the

Fed, given that the Fed makes loans that amount to more money than our national budget.*

The second solution is for each of the 50 states to do what North Dakota did about 90 years ago—create its own state-chartered and state-run bank. Because banks can be enormous profit centers, North Dakota started its own bank to inexpensively loan money to its farmers and small businesses; and when it does so (as it has all these years), all the profits from the interest paid go back into the state's coffers. This has a lot to do with why that state was among those least affected by the Bush financial crisis that began in 2008.

If every state did this, over time these state-run banks would provide strong competition to corporate banks, running many of them out of business or forcing them to operate more efficiently and to pay their CEOs less. State-run banks could also offer loans to citizens at a lower interest rate than the commercial banks, thus stimulating and stabilizing the states' local economies.†

---

*Interestingly, on May 6, 2010, two pieces of legislation were scheduled for a vote in the U.S. Senate, and both were expected to pass. One was a bill to audit the Fed, and the other was a bill to break up the six largest banks in America so none would be "too big to fail." Around 2:40 p.m. that day, the stock market suddenly dropped 998 points in a matter of a few minutes, with six stocks falling in value to a penny or less and one stock—Sotheby's—rising in value from around $33 per share to more than $100,000 per share. Five minutes later the market had largely recovered, but the shot across the bow by the large bankers wasn't missed by Congress or the White House.

That afternoon the president changed his mind, deciding to oppose both pieces of legislation, and that night the bill to break up the big banks (which control much of the trading on Wall Street) failed by 66 votes in the 100-member Senate. The bill to audit the Fed, after a meeting at the White House, was hastily rewritten that afternoon to limit the audit to a very narrow scope of the Fed's activities during the banking crisis of 2008.

†Ellen Brown has written extensively about these topics at her Web site, www.WebOfDebt.com.

Bring Back the STET

One of the biggest problems the United States has grappled with since the great waves of deregulation under Reagan and Clinton has been the bubblelike nature and the incredible velocity of the stock market. There is, however, a way to put a very small amount of sand into the stock market's gears, to borrow a phrase from economist Dean Baker, who has written on this topic, and thus stabilize both the markets and the economy.

We did it in the United States from 1914 to 1966 (and before that we did it to finance the Spanish-American War and the Civil War), and it's called the Securities Turnover Excise Tax (STET). For example, if we were to institute a 0.25 percent STET on every stock, swap, derivative, or other trade today, it would produce—in its first year—around $150 billion in revenue. Wall Street would be generating the money to fund its own bailout.

But there are other benefits as well.

As John Maynard Keynes pointed out in 1936 in his seminal economics tome *The General Theory of Employment, Interest, and Money,* such a securities transaction tax would have the effect of "mitigating the predominance of speculation over enterprise."[12]

In other words, it would tamp down toxic speculation while encouraging healthy investment. The reason is pretty straightforward: when there's no cost to trading, the behavior of Wall Street shifts from careful investment to careless gambling. The current system is like a casino where the house never makes any money and nobody's watching the players on closed-circuit TVs to prevent cheating.

A STET would, for instance, at least dampen if not deter the unethical tactics that are routinely employed these days. Consider one such scenario for a person or bank with lots of money or a huge line of credit: you buy a million shares of a particular stock over a day or two purely with the goal of driving up the stock's price (because everybody else sees all the buying activity and thinks they should jump onto the bandwagon) so that three days later you can sell all your stock at a profit and get out before its price collapses as the result of the sale.

Investment, on the other hand, is what happens when people buy stock because they believe the company has an underlying value. They're expecting the value to increase over time because the company has a good product or service and good management. Investment stabilizes markets, makes stock prices reflect real company value, and helps small investors securely build their own personal wealth over time.

Historically, from the founding of our country through the twentieth century, most people invested rather than speculated. When rules limiting speculation were gutted in the first big Republican deregulation binge during the administrations of Warren G. Harding, Calvin Coolidge, and Herbert Hoover (1921 to 1933), it created a speculative fever that caused the housing bubble of the early 1920s only to burst nationally starting in 1927 as housing values began to collapse. That housing collapse, which started in Florida, popped the stock market bubble and produced the Great Crash of 1929. That, in turn, crashed the national housing and stock markets and produced the Republican Great Depression of 1930 to 1942.

As part of the New Deal, Franklin D. Roosevelt put into place a series of rules to discourage speculation and promote investment, including maintaining—and doubling—the STET. Other countries followed our lead, and Australia, Austria, Belgium, Chile, China, France, Germany, Greece, India, Italy, Japan, Malaysia, and the United Kingdom all had or have STETs.

Reinstituting a STET now would generate money, so we wouldn't have to borrow it on the international market, as the Bush administration borrowed $700 billion (or more) from China, Saudi Arabia, and other countries and investors, adding to our national debt and saddling us with repaying it, with interest, at an actual cost of $1.4 trillion over 20 years.

So let's go back to what we know works. After Hoover's bail-out of the banks failed, FDR did a cold reboot of the entire system, putting into place strong rules to prevent speculative abuse. His doubling of the STET tax both produced revenue that more than funded the Securities and Exchange Commission and further prevented a repeat of the speculative bubble of the 1920s.

In the United Kingdom, a major campaign was launched in early 2010 to impose a variation on the STET—a 0.05% tax on interbank activities—that the British campaigners are calling the "Robin Hood Tax." Actor Ben Kingsley starred in a clever short video promoting the tax as a tiny charge on bankers but a boon for the public, enabling the funding of social programs and helping mitigate climate change.

We've done it before. We financed the Spanish-American War and partially financed the Civil War and World Wars I and II with STETs. We stabilized our stock market with a STET from the mid-1930s to 1966, and other nations are doing it today. It's time to do it again, this time using the STET to stop speculative behavior and so Wall Street can pay for its own bailout.

Don't Bank On the Banks

Banks should be thought of as public utilities, even if they're privately run. They exist to take deposits, facilitate commerce, and lend money to businesses and individuals. As such they shouldn't be in the business of gambling or speculating with other people's money. From the Glass-Steagall Act of 1933 until its 1999 repeal with the Gramm-Leach-Bliley Act (put forward by Republican senator Phil Gramm—there's that name again), banks could *not* get into the business of speculation.

After Phil Gramm's spectacular little bit of deregulation in 1999, banks went on a consolidation binge (we still weren't enforcing the Sherman Antitrust Act), with some buying up investment houses and others being bought *by* investment houses. The result was a speculative frenzy that nearly crashed the entire world banking system—and still may.

Because of this and another 2000 change in the law brought to us by Phil Gramm, it is currently perfectly legal for your bank to engage in what's called "proprietary trading"—and most all of the big national banks do. Proprietary trading is where the bank takes your deposits and, instead of loaning them out to your neighbors to buy a house or start a business, "invests" that money in the stock market, trading stocks, currencies, credit default swaps, and all manner of other things, minute-by-minute, hour-by-hour, 24 hours a day on superfast and highly sophisticated computer systems.

When the market is going up, your bank shows a huge profit and pays its traders and CEO millions. When the market goes down, your bank declares an emergency and gets bailed out by Congress and the Federal Deposit Insurance Corporation—and continues to pay its traders and CEO millions.

This is, frankly, insane. FDR was right: banks should be banks and nothing else. Nice boring businesses—green eyeshades and flannel suits, banker's hours, nothing exciting. It's your money, after all, that they're holding.

Until the day when the big banks are brought back under control, there are two alternatives.

Local Banks and Credit Unions

The first option is to move your money into local, community-oriented banks. These institutions are typically owned by one or more local people who—sometimes generations ago—set out to make money in the banking business. But because they're not national and they don't do bizarre things like proprietary trading or gambling in currency default swaps, they're generally pretty safe and stable. There's a movement—strongly publicized in 2010 by Arianna Huffington of the Huffington Post—to get individuals and government agencies to move their money from big banks into local community banks, and billions of dollars (including the accounts of some states and big unions) have been transferred as a result.

But still, even local community banks are for-profit operations. They often imitate the big banks when it comes to fees and interest rates because—just like the big banks—their primary reason for being in business is to make a profit. The upside is that the profit is going to *local* wealthy people. The downside is that it's going anywhere other than back to you.

So how can we get banking services—from checking accounts to mortgages to credit cards—without having to deal with a for-profit bank of *any* size?

The answer is community credit unions, which are depositor-owned financial institutions, run on a nonprofit basis, which do pretty much everything that a bank can do. When you give them your money to open a checking or savings account, you actually become a member of a nonprofit cooperative and can even run for a seat on the credit union's board of directors.

Breaking Your Bank

Community credit unions are answerable to their communities and usually use the profits from their bank-like operations to support local charities and to reduce the overall cost of the bank-like services they offer their depositors. And, just like banks, the federal government guarantees their deposits.

Community credit unions grew in membership by around 2 percent in 2009, a time when a lot of banks both big and small were shrinking or even collapsing. The Credit Union National Association (the trade association for credit unions) notes that in 2008 credit unions saved their members $9.2 billion that, had it been "earned" by banks (large or small), would instead have gone to banking corporation stockholders and CEOs.[13]

When Louise and I moved from Vermont to Portland, Oregon, the nearest bank branch to our home was owned by one of the six largest banks in the United States. The bank offered reasonable service and hours, but when they took billions in bailout money because of questionable activities that I'd call gambling, and their CEO and other senior executives continued to pay themselves millions in the face of obvious incompetence, we decided enough was enough.

We looked around Portland and discovered that there were more than 30 community credit unions in the area. While credit unions offer traditional banking services—from checking and savings accounts to credit cards to mortgages and car loans—they are owned by their members—not stockholders or local rich guys.

The idea of cooperative, locally owned, not-for-profit institutions getting into the banking business started in Germany in 1852, and the first U.S. credit union was opened in Manchester, New Hampshire, in 1908. Since then credit unions have spread across the country, and—particularly after the failure of so many savings-and-loan institutions after that industry was deregulated by the Reagan administration—many Americans have moved their money from banks or savings and loans into credit unions.

Louise and I did the same, as did others who are among my readers and radio listeners. Here's a note I received from a listener in 2010 that's quite enlightening and reflects in many ways our personal experience:[14]

> I found your New Years resolution very inspiring and vowed that I too would take my money out of Bank Against America and put it into a local credit union. I did some research and

found that Columbia Credit Union (right down the street from my house, no less) had a really good rating and had been voted "Grand Poobah Of Credit Unions" several years in a row. So I decided to go with that one. I had considered joining years ago when my wife was a member but, as soon as they told me they would have to do a credit check, I backed off. No sense in wasting everyone's time, I always say. But, as it turns out, they just wanted to be sure I didn't suck, they didn't really care if I was a few months overdue on my electric bill.

With that taken care of, I decided to give Bank Against America a couple of weeks to make sure everything had cleared. I went in fully intending to close my account but there was a phantom charge on the account and they couldn't close it until that cleared. I thought that was odd since I hadn't used the account in some time. They assured me it would clear the next day and I could find out the nature of the charge and close my account so I took out half of the money in the account and vowed to return the next day. The next day, the charge had cleared but they had no idea what the charge was and, as far as they could tell, there had been no charge, she said looking at me from the corner of her eye. I assumed that, if I tried closing the account, another phantom charge would suddenly appear so I took out all but eight dollars and decided I would let them send me monthly statements for the rest of my life and really get my $8 worth.

Well, two months later, I got a notice that my account was overdrawn, my account that I had not used since the end of January was overdrawn eighty cents. By the time I got to the bank the following Monday, it was overdrawn almost ten dollars. When I confronted the teller with the fact that I had not used the account in months and was told there were no monthly service charges, she agreed to waive the fees that should not have been charged in the first place. She then zeroed out the accounts and closed them for good.

I am now out from under the thumb of Bank Against America and am very happy with my credit union. I don't get my picture on my card, it doesn't have a groovy Autism Speaks symbol on it and they don't have a "Keep The Change" benefit, but I'm also not paying $5 for a money order while the CEOs get billions in bonuses and charge me $35 for going one cent over my balance. Thanks for the inspiration, Thom.

We can all move from the banksters to owning our own deposits, owning our own piece of a credit union. Try it, you'll like it!

CHAPTER **7**

Cool Our Fever

We live in a democracy and policies represent our collective will. We cannot blame others. If we allow the planet to pass tipping points...it will be hard to explain our role to our children. We cannot claim...that "we didn't know."

—Jim Hansen, Director, NASA Goddard
Institute for Space Studies[1]

I HAVE TAKEN THE FOUR-HOUR TRAIN RIDE FROM THE AIRPORT IN Frankfurt, Germany, to the Bavarian town of Stadtsteinach in the Frankenwald often enough to know it by heart. I look out the window and see the familiar sights—the towns, the rivers, the houses.

I have visited Stadtsteinach many times over the past 30 years, working with Salem International, a relief organization headquartered in that town. The community for abused kids that Louise and I founded in New Hampshire is based on its family-oriented model, and we have helped start Salem programs in Australia, Colombia, India, Israel, Peru, Russia, and Uganda, among others. So at least once a year I've made it back to Germany, and we lived there for a year in the mid-1980s.

But during the past decade, as the train rolls along eastward from Frankfurt, I've seen a dramatic change in the scenery and the landscape. First there were just a few: purplish-blue reflections, almost like deep, still water, covering large parts of the south-facing roofs as I looked north out the window of the train. Solar panels.

Then, over the next few years, the purplish-blue chunks began to spread all over, so now when I travel that route it seems like about a third—and in many towns even more—of all the roofs are covered with photovoltaic solar panels.

Given that Germany is one of the cloudiest countries in Europe, right up there with England—the sun shines for only about a third of the year—it seems crazy that it would have more solar panels per capita than any other country in the world and that it employs more than 40,000 people in the solar power industry. But the Germans made it happen.

They figured out a way to use their existing banking and power systems to begin to shift from dependence on coal and nuclear power to solar. And all it took were pretty small tweaks in the grand scheme of things. A minor recalibration in the way money moves around in the energy and banking sectors has turned the country into a solar powerhouse. Within the past decade, Germany has gone from near zero to producing 8,000 megawatts (MW) of power from solar, the equivalent capacity of eight nuclear power plants in the United States.

We can and should do the same—begin to invest in solar and other renewable forms of energy in America. For far too long, we have been hooked on oil, and we continue to pay a terrible price for it economically, politically, militarily, and environmentally. We need to wean ourselves from it both for our own future survival and prosperity and because so often other countries of the world look to us as an example of what they can or should do.

Strip Oil of Its Strategic Value

Two hundred years ago—and for a thousand years before that— one of the most strategic substances on earth was salt. It was "strategic" because no army could travel without it—salt was necessary to preserve food in a pre-refrigeration era. Wars were fought over it, and countries that had lots of salt made out well, while landlocked countries with no salt reserves were forced to sell their natural resources in exchange for it.

Oil is the new salt. It is now the planet's number one strategic resource. And, as has been noted by numerous commentators since the first Gulf War in 1990–1991, if the primary export of Iraq were broccoli, we wouldn't have given a damn that Saddam Hussein was a tin-pot tyrant.

The unfortunate reality is that we have within and around our national boundaries about 3 percent of the world's oil, but we consume about 24 percent of the world's produced oil. So we buy what we don't produce. This dependence represents a massive transfer of wealth from us to oil-producing countries. It's a strategic blunder that would have horrified Julius Caesar, who expanded the Roman Empire all the way to central Europe when he ran out of fuel—wood—by deforesting virtually all of Italy,* and then paid the price as his empire began to collapse from overexpansion.

Countries like Saudi Arabia rake in billions from oil-dependent countries like the United States, and oil revenues fuel their economies. In 2008, for instance, Saudi oil revenues spiked to $281 billion, a quadrupling of revenues from 2002. In 2009 those fell sharply to $115 billion, still nothing to sneeze at.[2] Oil revenues fund much of the fundamentalist Wahhabi Movement within Saudi Arabia, and it's out of this movement that come the

---

*The most conspicuous consequence of the deforestation of Italy during the early years of Caesar's rule was the "currency crisis" in which the cost of refining the silver used in Roman coins doubled—because the cost of the wood used to fire the smelters more than doubled. Some historians argue that this moment—when Rome could no longer supply its own energy needs—was the first signal of the beginning of the end of the Roman Empire. Interestingly, 1970 is widely accepted as the "peak oil" year for the United States, when our domestic supplies began an irreversible slide and our imports began to shoot up from 10 to 20 percent into the 50 to 60 percent range, where they are today. Then-president Richard Nixon called for an alternative energy strategy to get us off oil, and President Jimmy Carter actually put one into place in 1978, but Ronald Reagan rolled it back in 1981, leading directly to a dramatic increase in our imports of foreign oil.

most virulent anti-American and anti-Semitic rhetoric, textbooks, and television and radio programming.

Thirty years ago the nations composing OPEC, the Organization of Petroleum Exporting Countries, were producing around 30 million barrels per day, nearly half of the world's oil consumption. Regardless of how much we buy from OPEC nations or instead buy from Mexico, their production will continue, because oil is a fungible commodity, and it will just go to others who are no longer buying from whomever we choose to buy from. The proof of this is that today OPEC production is still around 30 million barrels—even though world oil consumption has increased and is now around 85 million barrels per day. The OPEC nations don't adjust production to meet demand; they maintain it to control prices so they have relatively stable income.

The only way we can change this situation is by reducing the amount of oil we use. Oil is a strategic commodity, and we need to strip it of its strategic value.

So what do we use all that oil for that makes it a strategic resource? We certainly don't use it to produce electricity—only 2 percent of our electricity is generated by oil because we have huge domestic supplies of coal, which produce more than half of our electricity. Pretty much nobody is producing electricity with oil except the oil-rich countries of the Middle East; even rapidly growing countries like China and India, for example, are not producing oil-fired power plants.

Thus, moving to solar, wind, biomass, or even nuclear power to generate electricity in the United States will help tremendously with our CO_2 output and all the pollution "externalities" associated with coal, but it will *not* make us less oil dependent or strip oil of its *strategic* significance.

The simple fact is that oil accounts for roughly 95 percent of the energy used for *transportation* in the United States (and our military is the world's single largest consumer of oil), and that's what makes it strategic. If we want to strip oil of its strategic value, so it can't be used as a weapon against us and we can use our remaining oil supplies for rational things like producing plastics and medicines, we need to shift our transportation sector away from oil and do so quickly.

This has been the essence of T. Boone Pickens's rant, although the eccentric oil billionaire is now a natural-gas billionaire, and he's suggesting that we convert our truck fleet in this country from oil to natural gas, which is nearly as bad a source of greenhouse gases as is oil. He's right that such a change would make us stronger and safer, both militarily and strategically, but he misses the climate change part of the equation (which is also increasingly becoming a strategic issue, as global climate deterioration leads to crises both at home and abroad).

Europe, Japan, and China are moving fast to shift their transportation sectors from oil to electricity, mostly through the use of trains. Brazil did it over the past 20 years by mandating that all cars and trucks sold would have to be "flex-fuel"—capable of burning gasoline or ethanol, diesel, or biodiesel. The result is that Brazil now meets nearly half of its transportation needs with domestically grown ethanol made from sugarcane, and more than 80 percent of its cars and trucks are now flex-fuel. And the added cost to Brazilian drivers to buy a flex-fuel car instead of a gasoline- or diesel-only car? About $100.

China is similarly moving in the direction of flex-fuel cars and is doubling every year its methanol production (mostly derived from domestically produced coal).

Flex-fuel cars can also burn part-ethanol, part-gasoline. If, for example, we were to shift to only 20 percent of automotive fuel being gasoline (the remainder being ethanol or methanol), a single gallon of gas would go five times as far. A 40-miles-per-gallon (mpg) car would become a 200 mpg car in terms of the strategic resource of oil-derived gasoline.

Most significantly, in the United States fully half of all automobiles are driven fewer than 20 miles in any given day. This is an easy range for an electric-only or a plug-in-hybrid car. By moving to the latter immediately—mandating them—we could shift the entire U.S. auto fleet to consuming 50 percent or more electricity instead of gas/diesel in less than a decade, stripping oil of half its strategic importance.

And our trade policies are *really* stupid on this. We have no import tariff whatsoever on oil, so there is nothing to discourage American drivers from using foreign-produced oil products to fuel their cars and trucks. But we charge an import tariff of more than $0.50 per gallon on ethanol, discouraging Americans from using the fuel and discouraging the more than 100 countries in the world where there's enough intense sunlight and sugarcane grows well from becoming net fuel exporters. And while we offer billions in tax breaks and incentives to oil, gas, and coal companies in the United States, we don't subsidize or support with tax subsidies (as the Danes are doing) electric or part-electric cars, either in their production or on the consumer end.

If we add to all of this some good scientific innovation in developing a mix of low-carbon energy resources (solar, biomass, geothermal, wind, tidal power) and can figure out a way to strip the carbon dioxide from our power plant smokestacks and turn it into a solid (calcium carbonate—which you can buy at the store under the brand name "Tums"—is a good candidate), it's not inconceivable that by 2050 we could cut our CO_2 emissions by more than 80 percent. And perhaps even decades sooner, if we begin now.[3] Plus we could strip oil of its strategic value and make our nation independent of Middle Eastern dictatorships.

So today we face a twofold crisis: First, the planet is getting warmer and it appears that our reliance on carbon-based fossil fuels is at the core of that trend. Second, the United States itself is more vulnerable to being held hostage by our reliance on imported fuel than we were in the early 1970s when the Arab oil embargo, triggered by our support of Israel in the Arab-Israeli War of 1973, nearly brought us to our knees.

Make Polluters Pay

In Denmark gasoline is taxed heavily and costs nearly $10 per gallon because the government—with the consent of its citizens, the result of a public information campaign that wasn't drowned out because there is no domestic oil industry to speak of—realized it was picking up about $3 per gallon of the real cost of gasoline.

Cars and trucks produce exhaust, which deteriorates buildings and statues, causes cancers and asthmas, and, when rain catches it on the way down, pollutes waterways and crops, with those poisons ending up in the food chain. With a national health-care system in addition to other public services, taxpayers in Denmark are picking up the cost of cleaning public areas and historic sites, treating the cancers and the asthmas, cleaning waterways, and restoring farmland that's been polluted by gas additives, like lead and MTBE (methyl tert-butyl ether).

So they decided to recover those "externalized costs" from gasoline with an increased gas tax.

Internalizing Profits while Externalizing Costs

Here in the United States, we allow businesses to externalize those costs and have government or consumers (in the case of cancers and asthma) pay for them, instead of incorporating that cost into the retail price of gas. The first imperative in business is to make a profit, and one of the effective ways to do so is to internalize profits while externalizing costs.

The internalizing-profits part is pretty easy to figure out: keep as much money as possible in the company, jack up prices to the maximum the market will bear, reduce expenses like labor and raw materials as much as possible, and increase efficiencies. All of these things constitute "the way of doing business" that most Americans understand.

But it's only half of the equation. "Externalizing costs" is a fancy way of saying, "Pass along the costs of doing business to consumers or to the government so that they don't affect profits."

Another part of this equation is the use of nature, which involves a bit of both internalizing to the company the "free" services of nature, including the presence of fossil fuels, and externalizing to nature the "costs" of pollution.

For example, a nuclear power plant must exhaust hundreds of millions of calories of "waste heat" every day. The way the nuclear industry does this is by building nuclear plants next to rivers or lakes, and cycling the cold water from "nature" through the nuke's cooling towers. Not only do nuclear power plants *not* pay for this water but the heat that's added into the rivers or lakes (and the water that escapes as steam, evaporated in huge plumes from the cooling towers) has a real set of "costs" associated with it.

Fish die, ecosystems are altered, and less water is available downstream for uses like drinking and agriculture. The same is true of the lethal radioactive nuclear waste that is produced at every nuclear plant, which is temporarily kept on-site and eventually shipped off to government-run waste management sites.

Not one of these costs is paid by nuclear power plant operators: instead, where they're run for-profit (like in the USA), it's the taxpayers, the citizens, and nature itself that pay the externalized cost.

The result is that we're wiping out nature by our use of its "free" resources. In 2001, with support from the United Nations, 1,360 of the world's top scientists and experts convened to examine the consequence on nature of these externalized costs. Four years later, after exhaustive analysis of ecosystems around the world, the Millennium Ecosystem Assessment was explicit:[4]

> Nearly two-thirds of the services provided by nature to human-
> kind are found to be in decline worldwide. In effect, the benefits

reaped from our engineering of the planet have been achieved by running down natural capital assets.

In many cases, it is literally a matter of living on borrowed time. By using up supplies of fresh ground water faster than can be recharged, for example, we are depleting assets at the expense of our children....

Unless we acknowledge the debt and prevent it from growing, we place in jeopardy the dreams of citizens everywhere to rid the world of hunger, extreme poverty, and avoidable disease— as well as increasing the risk of sudden changes to the planet's life-support systems from which even the wealthiest may not be shielded.

We also move into a world in which the variety of life becomes ever-more limited. The simpler, more uniform landscapes created by human activity have put thousands of species under the threat of extinction, affecting both the resilience of natural services and less tangible spiritual or cultural values.

We need to step back a bit from our oil, transportation, and energy policies and take a holistic view of the planet's ecology and how human actions affect it.

Earth as an Organism

Since the Gaia Hypothesis of James Lovelock, first popularized in his 1979 book,[5] the scientific and philosophical worlds are becoming increasingly aware that the planet earth is a single giant living organism, and all the living and "nonliving" parts of it are actually continually interacting in the dance we call life.

Our Aristotelian and Cartesian worldviews—that the world is actually a giant machine of sorts, and if we can just find the right lever to pull, we can fix everything—are being shown for the myths that they are, whether by climate change, the massive amount of oil that poured into the Gulf of Mexico in 2010, or the explosion of cancers and gender deformities in life forms worldwide (from frogs to humans) over the past 50 years as we've dumped huge amounts of hormone-mimicking plasticizers and other chemicals into our environment.

The simple reality is that I can take a car apart in my driveway, then put it back together, turn the key, and it'll run. But if I took a cow apart in my driveway, no matter how skilled a surgeon I am in reassembling it, it'll never moo again. Life is different from machines.

And our separation from life—whether by our worshiping gods in boxes every weekend, our belief in the supremacy of science, or our living, moving, and working in separated-from-life environments—has caused us to make personal and societal decisions that are destructive to life all around us for millennia. The tragic reality is that life is undergoing the sixth biggest extinction in the history of the planet—an extinction that may one day include us if we don't quickly wake up.

What we need to do immediately is to start taking small, incremental steps while also raising societal awareness in preparation for taking bigger and more substantive steps toward more earth-friendly approaches and policies when it comes to energy use.

The good news is that we know what we need to do to help solve our energy and sustainability problems.

For example, about 10 percent of the electricity we generate in the United States is consumed by "vampire" appliances and power supplies that are not even turned on or in use.[6] Another 6.5 percent of the electricity we produce in this country is wasted through "line losses"—the resistance of copper wires to the passage of electricity through them over long-line high-power transmission lines.[7] If we used electricity at the point of generation—like running your house off your own solar power—that loss percentage would drop to zero. Instead, because it's profitable for large power companies to have centralized generating stations, we're losing all that electricity as heat from transmission lines and are burning enormous amounts of coal, natural gas, and oil to produce it.

Lessons from Abroad

These problems are huge but they're not insurmountable. Other countries are already showing the way. Just as America now faces an unsustainable thirst for energy, so too was Germany faced with a power crisis in the late 1990s. Growing demands for electricity collided with the reality that the country has no oil reserves and a strong bias among its people against building new nuclear power plants in the wake of the nearby Chernobyl meltdown in 1986.

Yet the government knew that the country needed the electricity equivalent of at least one or two nuclear reactors over the next decade. So, how was it to generate that much electricity without nuclear power?

Germany's Alternative to Nuclear

In 1999 progressives in Germany passed the 100,000 Roof Program (Stromeinspeisungsgesetz),[8] which mandated that banks had to provide low-interest 10-year loans to homeowners sufficient for them to put solar panels on their houses. They then passed the Renewable Energies Law (Erneuerbare-Energien-Gesetz) and in 2004 integrated the 100,000 Roofs Program into it.[9] The Renewable Energies Law mandated that for the next 10 years the power company had to buy back power from those homeowners at a level substantially above the going rate so the homeowners' income from the solar panel would equal their loan payment on the panel and would also represent the actual cost to the power company to generate that amount of power had it built a new nuclear reactor.

At the end of the 10 years, the power company gets to buy solar power from its customers at its regular rate, and it now has a new source of power without having to pay to maintain (and eventually dismantle) a nuclear reactor. In fact, while the reactor would have had a 20- to 30-year lifespan, the solar panels typically have a lifespan of 50 years.

For the homeowners it was a no-brainer: they were getting low-interest loans from banks for the solar panels, and the power companies were paying for the power generated by those panels at a rate high enough to pay off the loans. It was like getting solar power panels for free.

If anything, the government underestimated how rapidly Germans would embrace the program and thus how much more power would be produced and how quickly. By 2007, Germany accounted for about half of the entire world's solar market. Just that one year, 2007, saw 1,300 MW of solar-generating capacity brought online across the country.[10]

For comparison, consider that the average generating capacity of each of the past five nuclear power plants brought online in the United States is 1,160 MW.[11]

In 2008, Germany added 2,000 MW of solar power to its grid, and in 2009 homeowners and businesses put onto their roofs enough solar panels to generate an additional 2,500 MW. Although the goal for the first decade of this century was to generate around 3,000 MW, eliminating the need to build two new nuclear power plants, this simple, no-risk program had instead added more than 8,500 MW of power.

And because the generation sources were scattered across the country, there was no need to run new high-tension power lines from central generating stations, making it more efficient and less expensive. Meanwhile, as dozens of German companies got into the business of manufacturing and installing solar power systems, the cost dropped by more than half between 1997 and 2007 and continues to plummet.[12]

The Germans expect that by 2050 more than 25 percent of their total electricity will come from solar (it's now just over 1 percent), adding to the roughly 12.5 percent of all German energy currently being produced by renewable sources (mostly hydro, but also including wind, biomass, and geothermal).[13]

The solar panel program has been so successful that the German government is now thinking that it's time to back off and leave this to the marketplace. As the *New York Times* noted in May 2008:[14]

> Thanks to its aggressive push into renewable energies, cloud-wreathed Germany has become an unlikely leader in the race to harness the sun's energy. It has by far the largest market for photovoltaic systems, which convert sunlight into electricity, with roughly half of the world's total installations....
>
> Now, though, with so many solar panels on so many rooftops, critics say Germany has too much of a good thing—even in a time of record oil prices. Conservative lawmakers, in particular, want to pare back generous government incentives that support solar development. They say solar generation is growing so fast that it threatens to overburden consumers with high electricity bills.

Translation: the solar panel manufacturers want the subsidies to stop so they can catch up with demand and then bump up the price—and the profits. Because of the subsidies, prices have been dropping faster than manufacturing costs.

Other Lessons from Europe

Germany is now considering incentives for its world-famous domestic auto industry to manufacture flex-fuel plug-in-hybrid automobiles that can get more than 500 mpg of (strategic) gasoline (boosted by domestically produced rooftop solar) with existing technology.

Meanwhile, Denmark has invested billions into having more than half of its entire auto fleet using only electricity by 2030.

Even China is no slouch when it comes to renewable energy. Although the Chinese continue to bring a dirty coal-fired power plant online about once a week, they surpassed every other nation in the world in 2010 in direct investment in the production of solar and wind power. As the *Los Angeles Times* reported in March 2010:[15]

> U.S. clean energy investments hit $18.6 billion last year, a report from the Pew Charitable Trusts said, a little more than half the Chinese total of $34.6 billion. Five years ago, China's investments in clean energy totaled just $2.5 billion.
>
> The United States also slipped behind 10 other countries, including Canada and Mexico, in clean energy investments as a share of the national economy....
>
> The Pew report pointed to another factor constraining U.S. competitiveness: a lack of national mandates for renewable energy production or a surcharge on greenhouse gas emissions that would make fossil fuels more expensive.

Clearly, it is time for the United States to take action.

It's the Taxes, Stupid

Taxes do two things. First and most obviously, they fund the operations of government. But far more importantly, taxes have been used since the founding of this country to encourage behaviors that we deem good for the nation and to discourage behaviors we consider bad.

For example, in 1793 Congress passed much of Alexander Hamilton's plan to use taxes—tariffs—on imported goods to encourage Americans to start manufacturing companies to meet demand and needs here in this country. Those tariffs stood until the 1980s, and American jobs stayed here along with them.

Similarly, two presidents—Republican Herbert Hoover (1929 to 1933) and Democrat Franklin D. Roosevelt (1933 to 1945)—supported high taxes on the rich. They believed it's not a good thing for too much wealth to be concentrated in too few hands because it would lead the wealthy to influence government policy for their own good rather than the public good.

So they taxed incomes above approximately $3 million per year (in today's dollars) at around 90 percent, and the effect of that tax from the 1930s until it was repealed by Ronald Reagan in the 1980s was that CEO pay in the United States was about the same as in the rest of the world—around 30 times that of the lowest-paid employee—and few families of dynastic wealth rose up to try to seize political power.

Other examples of using tax policies to promote public policy are the home mortgage interest deduction (which encourages home ownership) and providing accelerated deductibility to companies for research and development.

Taxing Carbon

Now we need a new tax to encourage change that will help us kick our addiction to oil and spur us toward a clean-energy future. We need a tax on carbon. Other countries are already doing it in a variety of direct and indirect ways. This simple solution will address both the environmental problem of carbon-based fuels fouling our atmosphere and the strategic problem of our transportation system's being the weakness that keeps us addicted to imported oil.

There are two pretty straightforward ways to tax carbon. The first is to simply assign a tariff or tax value to it at any particular point in its use cycle. The tax could be levied when it's used, for example, or when it's extracted. A tax on carbon that's imported would serve to really speed our change from gasoline-only cars to flex-fuel and plug-in-hybrid cars.

The second way to tax carbon is to tax the industrial emission of it but also "allow" a certain amount of carbon to be released into the atmosphere by "giving away" to polluters what are referred to as "carbon credits." A threshold is set for the total amount of carbon a country will allow to be emitted (a "cap"), and anything above that point is heavily taxed. Companies that don't want to pay the tax can instead pay to buy carbon-emitting credits from companies that have a surplus of them (presumably because they've reduced their levels of carbon pollution), thus "trading" the carbon credits.

This cap-and-trade program can work if the threshold is low enough, the number of credits "given away" is low enough, and the tax is high enough. On the other hand, if the thresholds are set high, the taxes are low, and the majority of the credits are given away, cap-and-trade policy becomes a windfall for Wall Street (the credits are traded via conventional commodity exchange mechanisms) but doesn't do much for reducing carbon emissions.

The European Union, for example, has instituted a cap-and-trade program, although many European countries (Denmark is the leader) have gone one better by instituting domestic carbon or oil taxes to further encourage conservation, innovation, and the development of domestic renewables.

We should do the same.

One problem with this is that, in the absence of tariffs, many companies will simply export more manufacturing jobs to the few countries in the world that are not taxing carbon so that they can continue to use carbon-based fuels (or electricity generated from them) *over there* instead of here.

But there is a way around this. We can extend our carbon tax throughout the chain of manufacture. Just like our tariffs used to be based, in part, on the relative cost of foreign labor, a carbon tax tariff could be based on the amount of carbon generated in the manufacture of goods overseas. A carbon-based value-added-tax (VAT), where a small tax is imposed at every stage of manufacture reflecting the carbon used to bring about that manufacture, would do the job quite nicely if it had the power to extend itself to imported goods.

Of course, this is what the oilmen who fund the right-wing protest movements fear the most. But their interests are not those of the United States of America. And the faster Americans realize that, the better.

CHAPTER **8**

They Will Steal It!

War will exist until that distant day when the conscientious
objector enjoys the same reputation and prestige that the
warrior does today.

—John F. Kennedy

IN 1981, IN THE MIDST OF A WIDE-RANGING CONVERSATION DUR-
ing a night flight across the Atlantic, I got one of the biggest foreign policy insights of my life. Ever since I heard it, it's filtered
my observations of the behavior of virtually every country in the
world, particularly ours.

I'd gone to Uganda in 1980 to help start a program to feed the
tens of thousands of people starving as a result of the 1978–1979
war, started when Uganda's neighbor to the south, Tanzania, finally said "Enough!" to the atrocities perpetuated by Ugandan
dictator Idi Amin and invaded the country. They drove Amin out
(he went to Libya first, then to Saudi Arabia, where he lived to a
ripe old age in a palace, courtesy of the king and our oil dollars),
but the Uganda-Tanzania War produced a disaster for the people
of Uganda.

Our relief program was up and running, at least in infant
form (it's still there and operating), and African-American comedian and activist Dick Gregory agreed to go to Uganda with
me to see it and to help publicize the starvation so we could raise
funds in the United States to expand the program. As the two of
us crossed the Atlantic, his first trip to the African continent and
my third or fourth, we sat in the plane and drank red wine and

talked of all sorts of things, including our common opposition to the Vietnam War back in the day.

In the middle of our discussion about the United States and its unfortunate military adventures abroad, Dick dropped on me the most profound comment I've ever heard about foreign policy and human nature: "I don't know why America always thinks she has to run all around the world forcing people to take our way of governance at the barrel of a gun," he said. He paused for a sip of wine, and then added with a sly grin, "When you've got something really good, you don't have to force it on people. *They will steal it!*"

World history from (and before) the founding of our nation validates that assertion. When the United States was founded, it was seen by the kingdoms and the theocracies of Europe as a fragile experiment all but doomed to fail. Alexis de Tocqueville, a young French nobleman and historian, visited America for six months in the early 1830s and wrote a portrait of our country titled *Democracy in America.** He was frankly skeptical but hopeful that we could make it work.

When in the 1860s we descended into the long and bloody Civil War, the rest of the world held its breath. The experiment here, the very *idea* of America, was going to fail, or so it appeared. But we emerged from it stronger and more unified than before, and in the seven generations since then we have extended the Enlightenment notions of egalitarianism and democracy on which our country was founded to African Americans (and other minorities) and to women.

It is no accident that while there were arguably a handful of "democratic" nations at the time of our Civil War, there are around a hundred countries in the world today that claim that system of governance. Only two—Germany and Japan—did so

---

Democracy in America is the name by which this work is most commonly known, and that is the title of later printings. The original work, published in 1835, was titled *The Republic of the United States of America, and Its Political Institutions, Reviewed and Examined.*

after we defeated them militarily. (The jury is still out on Iraq and Afghanistan.) The rest "stole" our good idea and made it their own—and many have actually improved on it, with strong social safety nets and political systems of proportional representation or variations on instant runoff voting.

Here's the irony: We came to believe in the concepts of freedom, egalitarianism, justice, tolerance, and democracy without being forced to do so, and yet we repeatedly try to force that on others. Our military budget today is larger than that of every other country in the world—*combined.* Since World War II, we've been stuck in a rut that two of our presidents—Dwight D. Eisenhower and John F. Kennedy—explicitly warned us about, of relying on our military to help make the world safe for its democracies.

The saner and smarter alternative, the higher road we need to be taking, is best demonstrated by the work of a man named Greg Mortenson.

In 1993, Mortenson attempted to climb K2, the world's second-highest mountain in the remote tribal area of northern Pakistan. Unfortunately, he was involved in an ordeal trying to rescue a fellow climber. On his descent, he became weak and exhausted and ended up in a small village, where people took him in and for months—despite a poverty so severe they couldn't even afford to have a school in their little community—cared for his wounds, fed him, and housed him until he could return to America.

Mortenson set out to repay the debt of hospitality he'd incurred in Pakistan by building the community a school. It took some time and rather Herculean efforts, but he did it, and he has now raised enough money to build more than 130 such small schools in remote areas of northwestern Pakistan and, most recently, Afghanistan.

These areas, with their hospitality- and obligation-based cultures, are the epicenter of the Taliban. Yet in the places where Mortenson has built schools, people are friendly to Americans and reject the virulent anti-Americanism the Taliban is promoting;

five of Mortenson's teachers are former Taliban. By helping provide education, especially to girls, who previously were prohibited from studying, Mortenson has both elevated the quality of life (along with the status of women) and created a debt of obligation from them to us.

Mortenson wrote two best-selling books about his experiences, *Three Cups of Tea: One Man's Mission to Promote Peace One School at a Time* and a sequel, *Stones into Schools: Promoting Peace with Books, Not Bombs, in Afghanistan and Pakistan.*[1] In both, with vivid prose and a compelling story, he illustrates the wisdom of what can be achieved through civic, not military, engagement. Mortenson's schools are, in fact, "promoting peace with books, not bombs."

That is the face of America we want the world to see, the face of enlightened change for the better.

But not far from Mortenson's schools, American bombs rained on villages, often mistaking wedding parties or other social gatherings as military operations, killing innocent civilians and creating a blood debt of vengeance against us.

And, ironically, the cost of a single cruise missile—we've deployed hundreds into the region and in the process killed thousands of innocent civilians—could have instead paid for the construction and the furnishing of 20 schools.

So the face of America that the world sees, more often than not, is a harsh militaristic one and not a diplomatic one. We now have a bloated military with troops and bases all over the world, and we use them far too often—just because they are there.

Abraham Maslow, the founder of humanistic psychology, often said words to the effect that "If the only tool you have is a hammer, every problem looks like a nail." We've been using the hammer of military power to solve problems that, arguably, *began* because of our use of military power to defend despots in natural-resource-rich (principally oil) regions. As we saw in the previous chapter, we need to kick our addiction to oil, which in itself will reduce our need for military operations worldwide.

We also desperately need to take other measures as well. We can cut our "defense" spending drastically and redirect those resources, close most of our foreign bases and bring our troops home, and bring back the draft so that all Americans—not just the poor—have the experience and an understanding of the military.

Return Our Military to Jefferson's Vision

Many of the world's mature democracies require every high-school graduate to serve a year or two of either military or civil service. At first blush this may seem oppressive, but history shows it's actually one of the best ways to prevent a military from becoming its own insular and dangerous subculture, to prevent the lower ranks from being overwhelmed by people trying to escape poverty, and to keep military actions accountable to the people.

Many of our country's Founders argued strongly against a standing army during times of peace, although they favored a navy to protect our shoreline borders (and would likely favor an air force if they had one). They believed that an army had too much potential for mischief—to oppress people or even to stage a military coup and take over an elected government, something that happened three times in Pakistan's 63-year history as a nation and which has happened in numerous other nations over the past few centuries.

Thomas Jefferson first suggested not having a standing army, and he wrote a series of letters in 1787, as the Constitution was being debated, urging James Madison and others to write it into the Constitution. He suggested three provisions: a constitutional ban on a standing army, a provision making every able-bodied male a trained member of a local militia that could come under national control if the country was attacked, and a provision making sure every male had a weapon handy at home if that day ever came.

When Jefferson received the first draft of the new Constitution in 1787, he wrote that without a Bill of Rights he would recommend that Virginia oppose it. In a February 1788 letter, he noted to his friend C. W. F. Dumas:[2]

> With respect to the new Government, nine or ten States will probably have accepted by the end of this month. The others may oppose it. Virginia, I think, will be of this number. Besides other objections of less moment, she will insist on annexing a bill of rights to the new Constitution, i.e. a bill wherein the government shall declare that, 1. Religion shall be free; 2. Printing presses free; 3. Trials by jury preserved in all cases; 4. No monopolies in commerce; 5. No standing army. Upon receiving this bill of rights, she will probably depart from her other objections...

The topic was hotly debated, and Alexander Hamilton wrote an extensive article about it, first published in the *Daily Advertiser* on January 10, 1788, an article now known as No. 29 of the Federalist Papers:[3]

> If standing armies are dangerous to liberty, an efficacious power over the militia, in the body to whose care the protection of the State is committed, ought, as far as possible, to take away the inducement and the pretext to such unfriendly institutions....

> [A citizens' militia] appears to me the only substitute that can be devised for a standing army, and the best possible security against it...

But while many Founders saw a standing army as a threat to democracy, others pointed to threats ranging from hostile Indians to French Canadians and Spanish Floridians as reasons to keep it. The debates led to a clumsy compromise, with the ban on a standing army and a universal requirement for membership in a militia chopped away, to be revisited at a future date. The tattered and compromised remnant of that discussion is today known as the

Second Amendment, which reads, in its entirety: "A well regulated militia, being necessary to the security of a free state, the right of the people to keep and bear arms, shall not be infringed."*

After he became president in 1801, Jefferson again tried to revive his argument. He slashed the size of the army from a quarter million to just over 3,000 soldiers, closing forts and cutting costs. But he couldn't kill off the army altogether because the citizens' militia had never been formalized at a federal level (and there were still those nasty "Indian Wars" going on). After he left office in 1809, Jefferson concluded that if he couldn't get rid of the army, every man should be a member of it, if only for a brief time. This would ensure a diversity of opinions in the army and would minimize the chances of an entrenched military culture that could become so powerful as to stage a coup or tempt the president into playing commander-in-chief too often in foreign adventures.

Jefferson was also morally offended by the idea of an army that people would join only because they were too poor to afford an education and a job. For such people he wanted universal free public education, including free college tuition, which he brought into being when he founded the University of Virginia.

In a June 1813 letter to his old friend (and future president) James Monroe, he wrote:[4]

> It is more a subject of joy that we have so few of the desperate characters which compose modern regular armies. But it proves more forcibly the necessity of obliging every citizen to be a soldier; this was the case with the Greeks and Romans, and must be that of every free State. Where there is no oppression there will be no pauper hirelings.

As history shows, Jefferson was more often right than wrong.

---

*Clearly, the intent of the Second Amendment was not to have citizens protect themselves from an oppressive government, nor was it based on the "right to self-defense in your own home" argument put forth by the National Rifle Association and other advocates of ownership of assault weapons.

Bring Back the Draft

The idea of avoiding "pauper hirelings" by instituting a system of citizen-soldiers is what we would now call a military draft. We should institute a universal draft, with a strong public service option—from planting trees to assisting in schools to helping in hospitals—easily and readily available for those young people who don't want to go into the military.

The result will be a generation of citizens who feel more bonded with and committed to their nation, who have experienced the critical developmental stage of a "rite of passage" into adulthood, and who have experienced more of America and the world than just their own neighborhood.

Universal service would also help calm President Eisenhower's fears. The old general left us the following warning as he departed from office in 1960:[5]

> In the councils of government, we must guard against the acquisition of unwarranted influence, whether sought or unsought, by the military-industrial complex. The potential for the disastrous rise of misplaced power exists and will persist.
>
> We must never let the weight of this combination endanger our liberties or democratic processes. We should take nothing for granted.

And, as President Herbert Hoover (1929 to 1933) correctly noted, "Old men declare war. But it's the youth who must fight and die." When the children of our president, vice president, and members of Congress are all obliged to serve, the odds are infinitely higher that our leaders won't speak so glibly about the acceptability of "a few casualties" in optional wars of choice like Iraq.

By including women and by adding a very broad government-funded option of national public service, we can bring about a modern version of Jefferson's vision and create both a more egalitarian society and a less belligerent and poverty-driven military.

Downsize the Pentagon

On April 15, 2010, Glenn Beck did a rather remarkable thing on his Fox "News" TV show. He pointed out that our military is stretched all over the world and that the United States spends 47 percent of the military spending of *the entire world,* and he called for cutting in half our annual $700 billion–plus military budget. We don't need a military with outposts in Germany and Japan and pretty much everywhere else—the military of an empire—because, Beck said, "We are not an empire; we are a republic."

Up until recently there had basically been, at least in the public mind, only two types of people who had strong opinions about military budgets: "hawks" who want a "strong national defense," and "doves" (aka "hippies") who want "peace" and therefore don't want much military at all. Now, with the continuing infiltration of libertarian and classical conservative ideas into the Republican Party, a new breed of right-wing populist is emerging who sees our bloated defense budget as wasteful and unnecessary.

Consider that just during the eight years of the Bush-Cheney administration—while they were doubling the national debt from around $5 trillion to around $12 trillion—annual defense spending just about doubled, with the majority of that extra spending going to "contractors" (mostly Cheney's old company Halliburton and other Bush family cronies) as more and more military and government functions were privatized.

Back when Reagan was doing the same thing Bush Jr. did—borrowing and spending on the military, particularly directing huge amounts of money to donors and cronies*—it was rationalized as a way of "making us stronger" *and* as a stimulus to the nation's economy. Just look at all those jobs building bombs and the

---

*In Reagan's case it was hundreds of billions (trillions in today's money) spent on "Star Wars," with most of it going to companies that were big supporters of his or were headed by former officials from the Nixon and Reagan administrations.

missiles to deliver them! But the problem with spending money on a bomb is that when that bomb is dropped on somebody (or retired to the scrap heap), the money vanishes.

But if the same money is spent on high-speed rail or schools or other physical or intellectual infrastructure (research, for example), it comes back to society and the government over and over again in the form of a more vibrant economy and a more well-paid (and thus higher tax-paying) workforce.

This is, of course, the argument real "doves" have been making since the founding of this country—that we can actually be stronger as a nation, in terms of both national defense and a vibrant economy, by spending less on defense. It's nice to hear that "conservatives" and "libertarians" have finally caught on.

For example, in 2009, Benjamin Friedman of the Cato Institute, a libertarian think tank, wrote in the *Christian Science Monitor:*[6]

> To really keep us safe, we should slash defense spending. Americans should prepare for fewer wars, not different ones. Far from providing our defense, our military posture endangers us. It drags us into others' conflicts, provokes animosity, and wastes resources. We need a defense budget worthy of the name. We need military restraint. And that would allow us to cut defense spending roughly in half.

Instead of rational policies like this—which for the past half-century have been advocated by "doves" from President Eisenhower to Students for a Democratic Society founder Tom Hayden—we have been in the thrall of a military-industrial-media-lobbying complex that has been sucking the blood of this nation for generations, both figuratively and literally.

The peak result of that was seen during the Bush-Cheney administration, when senior officials actually turned their backs on previous American presidents and policy, from George Washington through Bill Clinton, and pushed our military to invade a country that presented no threat to us, kill hundreds of thousands of innocent civilians, and torture (to the point of death in as many as 100 cases) "suspects."

Break the Cycle Now

Remember the Arnold Schwarzenegger action movies and the John Wayne westerns? Someone would stick a gun in the bad guy's face, and he would break down and start blubbering, "Yeah, I did it." Perry Mason was more successful than Arnold or John. He used psychology.

In a June 2005 *Atlantic* magazine article, Stephen Budiansky wrote about Marine Major Sherwood Moran, the most successful interrogator of Japanese prisoners of war during World War II. He spoke Japanese, he lived in Japan, and he knew the culture. He believed that the "'first and most important victory' is getting 'into the mind and into the heart' of the prisoner and achieving an 'intellectual and spiritual' rapport with him."[7]

When the 1993 movie *Schindler's List* came out, we were living in Atlanta and living with us was Oliver, a 16-year-old German exchange student. Oliver, who had been through the German public schools and was a high school student, went with us to see it, and midway through the movie he broke down and sobbed; he cried the rest of the way through that movie and for an hour as we drove home. When he could finally talk about it, he said: "I knew we did that stuff. We learned that in school. But I didn't really, *really* know we did that stuff—until I saw the movie."

When we lived in Germany, we used to go on daytrips and weekly excursions with our kids. We went to the Dachau concentration camp, where Sigmund Rascher performed his experiments on people, many of whom died. We walked through Dachau with our children, and looked at pictures of the people, the bodies stacked up to be put in the crematorium, and we walked among the furnaces.

I wonder when the day will come that a generation of Americans will walk through a museum at the Bagram Air Force Base in Afghanistan, or Abu Ghraib in Iraq, or Guantánamo in Cuba, or perhaps one of the hidden detention sites inside the United States or in Poland or in Czechoslovakia, and view it as our Dachau—places where horrific acts took place.

And we will walk through those museums with our children, saying, "Yes, that's what we did. This is what George Bush, Alberto Gonzalez, and Dick Cheney did. And we are ashamed."

A Bush administration Schindler's List, about the torture and the killings carried out in our name, under the guise of promoting democracy and bringing peace:

- 1 million dead in Iraq

- 4.5 million Iraqi refugees

- Iraqi children prostituting themselves because their parents are dead

- 5 million Iraqi orphans

- Tortured Iraqi prisoners

- Aerial bombardment and murder of wedding parties and civilians in Afghanistan and Pakistan

And on that future day, when a film is made about America's killing and torturing human beings, I wonder if our children and grandchildren will watch the movie and break down sobbing as Oliver did.

Moving Forward

We can ensure that there are no more such atrocities done in our name by taking a series of simple, straightforward measures: cutting our defense budget in half, bringing our military forces home from bases overseas, and instituting a national service program so that every American feels that he or she has a stake when a president or Congress decides to go off on some foreign military adventure.

We need to stop dropping bombs to promote freedom and democracy and start engaging, educating, and enlightening others so that they can see the fundamental goodness of the traditional American virtues of a free and open society.

CHAPTER 9

Put Lou Dobbs out to Pasture

Only a fool would try to deprive working men and working women of their right to join the union of their choice.

—Dwight D. Eisenhower

Back in the late 1980s, when I ran an advertising agency in Atlanta, a multinational corporation approached us about producing its internal newsletter, a monthly eight-pager about the company's goings-on in the United States, Mexico, and Japan. Not surprisingly, they wanted the newsletter produced in English, Spanish, and Japanese.

For our small agency trolling for clients, this corporation was a big fish—it could provide a good shot of cash for what was then a startup business with a half dozen employees—so I put a help-wanted ad in the local daily newspaper, the *Atlanta Constitution-Journal,* for a graphic designer who was also fluent enough in those three languages to know how to set type and where to hyphenate words (the company was providing us with the text in the three languages). It was clearly a search for a needle in a haystack, so I was totally shocked when a young man showed up on our doorstep, claiming that he was a graphic artist with fluency in all three languages.

Hiroki (not his real name), the son of Japanese immigrants, had been born in Japan and spoke Japanese at home. When he was a young boy, his family moved to a major South American city, and he lived there until his last year of high school, acquiring the Spanish language along the way. Then his father's job brought him to Atlanta, where Hiroki finished high school and spent four years in college getting a degree in graphic arts. As a recent grad, he was looking for his first job in America.

There was one problem, however: Hiroki was not a U.S. citizen and didn't have legal permission to work in the United States. To get a job, both he and his employer (me) would have to prove to the Immigration and Naturalization Service (INS, now part of the Department of Homeland Security) that he had skills no American could offer.

He filled out his form for a visa, and I wrote a letter stating that I could not find an American citizen who was a graphic designer *and* spoke those three languages. A few weeks passed, while I assured the corporate client that we *would* be able to do the job. Then a man from the INS called me and pressed me quite hard—saying that they may even inspect my workplace—on whether I really couldn't find an American graphic designer in Atlanta who was fluent in those three languages.

He then asked what I would be paying Hiroki, making it plain that the visa would be denied if I was hiring him only so that I could pay him less than what I would have to pay an American. I assured him that Hiroki would start out at the same pay as our other designers and would have the same advancement potentials they had.

Hiroki got a call with similar questions and had to go to the INS office in Atlanta to make his plea. While he was there, they called me again to confirm what he was saying, warning me again that if we paid him a lesser wage than we'd pay an American, there could be criminal penalties.

Hiroki got the visa, we got the newsletter job, and our business grew. Hiroki was with us for years, becoming one of our best designers and a great employee.

There's a good reason why the government officials were suspicious that I would hire an immigrant to bring down the cost of doing business, which would boost my profits: it's a common practice among businesses small and large. In fact, it is the single most important factor in our "immigration problem"—employers hiring "illegal immigrants" or "undocumented workers" (take your pick) because they will work for less money than American workers.

In other words, our problem is not an immigration issue, it's an *economic* one.

And the way to address it is to crack down—hard!—on businesses that break the law and hire people who do not have a work permit and so will work illegally for substandard wages. Once you stop employers from hiring illegal workers, you stanch the flow of immigrants crossing our borders illegally.

The same corporate lust for profits is at work in the whole "outsourcing" business—instead of paying substandard wages here, they're doing it over there. Outsourcing is not about some high-and-mighty notion of creating a competitive "global marketplace"—it's about corporations shipping jobs to places where they can pay slave wages to benefit their bottom line.

The Outsourcing Mania

Around the time I hired Hiroki, General Electric's then-CEO Jack Welch made a trip to India to pitch some GE business and stumbled upon something big. Looking around at a well-educated and skilled workforce that spoke English and—most important—was willing to work for a few dollars an hour, he realized the bonanza this could represent for GE, which was paying back-office bookkeepers and customer support workers in America $20 or more per hour with benefits.

It was a "Eureka!" moment for Welch, and he proudly claims to be the grandfather of the modern movement of outsourcing pink- and white-collar jobs to India (and other English-speaking countries like the Philippines).

On his Web site, Welch includes a Q&A with him that was published in *Business Week* on July 31, 2006:[1]

> *How can we change things in the U.S. so we don't have to out-source to India and other countries anymore?*
>
> We can't—and we shouldn't.
>
> Look, the debate over outsourcing should be over by now. It was pretty much all about politics to begin with. The question now is not how do we stop outsourcing, but how do we use outsourcing to enhance competitiveness in what is, and forever will be, a global marketplace?
>
> Of course, outsourcing has not been painless: Layoffs hurt. Still, they have to be seen as part of a broader picture, one in which outsourcing is not only integral to the world economy but crucial to our own growth.
>
> Integral because economies always respond to consumer demands. People have come to expect the lowest price and the highest quality in one package. And companies can't deliver on that expectation without moving around the world to capture cost advantages and innovative minds.

He concludes his answer with this depressing kick-in-the-face to American workers: "So forget outsourcing. America's labor challenge today is talent insourcing."

Welch is cut from the same cloth as Alan Greenspan, the Ronald Reagan–appointed Federal Reserve Chairman, a devotee of Ayn Rand and a promoter of outsourcing as well as "talent insourcing." Greenspan believed that one of our big problems was "wage inflation," a term he applied only to the earnings of working-class people and never to the stratospheric salaries paid to CEOs and other corporate executives.

In a September 2007 interview on C-SPAN for *Book TV,* Greenspan said:[2]

> We pay the highest skilled-labor wages in the world. If we would open up our borders to skilled labor far more than we do, we would attract a very substantial quantity of skilled labor which would suppress the wage levels of the skilled because the skilled are essentially being subsidized by the government, meaning our competition is being kept outside the country.

Easy to say—if you're so incredibly wealthy that neither you nor your children or grandchildren will ever need a job answering phones or doing bookkeeping or being an engineer.

Under the guise of satisfying a consumer demand for low prices, multinationals have accelerated outsourcing ever since the Reagan years and pushed the "free trade" and "globalization" ideology that has given us the NAFTA and GATT/WTO processes initiated under President George H. W. Bush and finished by President Bill Clinton. As a direct result, American blue-collar workers saw their jobs vanish as factories making things from jeans to precision tools moved to Mexico and other countries. Not to worry, the Bush and Clinton administrations assured workers, just learn new skills so you can join the "service economy," which included millions of new "Do you want fries with that?" and "Welcome to Wal-Mart" jobs, and the wonderful new Internet that would bring millions of new computer software and hardware engineering jobs to America.

It seemed to work for a few years, helped along by a dot-com bubble, followed by a credit bubble, and then a housing bubble. But when the bubbles all burst, American blue-collar workers (who are increasingly showing up at Tea Party rallies and joining citizens' militias) realized they were screwed, and the pink- and white-collar workers who thought their jobs were secure (and so didn't get all militant in the 1980s and 1990s like the blue-collar union men and women) discovered that they were screwed, too.

So Jack Welch can talk all he wants about how we can "use outsourcing to enhance competitiveness" in the "global market-place," but that can't stand the light of day.

One illuminating glimpse of what that outsourced "competition" looks like today comes to us via a story published in London's *Daily Mail* on April 18, 2010, headlined: "The Image Microsoft Doesn't Want You to See: Too Tired to Stay Awake, the Chinese Workers Earning Just 34p an Hour." The accompanying photograph, smuggled out of a Chinese factory run by KYE Systems at Dongguan, China, showed workers passed out from exhaustion while still on the assembly line—a line producing goods for Microsoft, Hewlett-Packard, Samsung, Acer, and Logitech, among other companies. The article noted:[3]

> The mostly female workers, aged 18 to 25, work from 7:45 am to 10:55 pm, sometimes with 1,000 workers crammed into one 105 foot by 105 foot room.
>
> They are not allowed to talk or listen to music, are forced to eat substandard meals from the factory cafeterias, have no bathroom breaks during their shifts and must clean the toilets as discipline, according to the NLC [National Labor Committee].
>
> The workers also sleep on site, in factory dormitories, with 14 workers to a room. They must buy their own mattresses and bedding, or else sleep on 28-inch-wide plywood boards. They "shower" with a sponge and a bucket.
>
> And many of the workers, because they are young women, are regularly sexually harassed, the NLC claimed.

The article continues with the story of one woman who was fired after she lost a finger to a hole-punching machine, and another who said, "We are like prisoners." They are paid about $25 per week, according to the article.

How Jack Welch, Bill Clinton, or the oracle at the *New York Times,* Thomas Friedman, think American workers can ever "compete" with such conditions and circumstances in the "flat world" that Friedman lauds is beyond comprehension. This "outsourcing is good" and "free trade" ideology obviously aids the class of people who are executives in or stockholders of transnational corporations, but what possible gain is in it for the workers in any nation?

The answer, according to such elitists, is that it provides "more freedom" for American "consumers" because they now have more choices of cheaper goods. But that ideology treats us only as consumers instead of citizens and assumes that our buying options are so important to us that we would ignore what this means for our income, our quality-of-life, our ethics, or our responsibility as citizens to the future of our nation.

These, however, are discussions you will *not* hear on the network Jack Welch used to run (NBC)—or any other corporate or corporate-sponsored (like PBS) network in today's media world. An examination of the nature of outsourcing—and its long-term effects on our quality of life here—would illuminate the real winners and losers in this new "flat world," and that's never to happen.

Instead they want to direct all our anger and frustration about losing our jobs against all those brown people—particularly the ones coming in from Mexico and countries south of us—and have us conclude that it's the *immigrants* who are to blame.

And it's an easy story line to cover and promote regularly in the news, because—like most things used to misdirect us from the real agenda (think of "weapons of mass destruction" in Iraq instead of Cheney's note that "Iraq sits on top of 10 percent of the world's oil"[4])—there's a kernel of truth under the larger issue.

So an interesting rift has taken place within the GOP regarding the whole immigration issue—between the corporatist Republicans ("Amnesty!") and the racist Republicans ("Fence!"). And it provides an opportunity for progressives to step forward with some clear solutions that address not only the immigration problem facing America but also the labor and wages problems that are decimating our middle class.

The solutions lie in following the strategies that brought us sustained success in creating a stable middle class in the midtwentieth century.

Looking Back to Look Ahead

When the topic of illegal immigration comes up, we hear this recurring mantra: "There are some jobs Americans won't do."

It's a lie.

Americans will do virtually any legal job if they're paid a decent wage. This is the economic reality underlying the immigration debate.

The history of the labor struggle in America has always been about securing wages and benefits that provide a decent living for workers and their families. And the best way to guarantee that is by making sure the labor market is not flooded. Working Americans have always known this simple equation: more workers, lower wages; fewer workers, higher wages.

Progressives fought—and many lost their lives in the battle—to limit the pool of "labor-hours" available to the robber barons from the 1870s through the 1930s, and their successes created the modern middle class:

- They limited labor-hours by pushing for the 50-hour week and the 10-hour day (and then later the 40-hour week and the 8-hour day).

- They limited labor-hours by pushing for laws against child labor (which competed with adult labor).

- They limited labor-hours by working for passage of the landmark 1935 National Labor Relations Act (aka the Wagner Act) that provided for union shops in the private sector.

- They limited labor-hours by supporting laws that would regulate immigration into the United States to a small enough flow that it wouldn't dilute the unionized labor pool.

As Wikipedia noted in early 2010: "The first laws creating a quota for immigrants were passed in the 1920s, in response to a sense that the country could no longer absorb large numbers of unskilled workers, despite pleas by big business that it wanted the new workers."

Even as major a labor figure as César Chávez, the co-founder of the United Farm Workers (UFW) union, fought against illegal immigration, and the UFW turned in undocumented workers during his tenure as president. Chávez, like progressives since the 1870s, understood the simple reality that labor rises and falls in price as a function of availability. In 1969, Chávez led a march to the Mexican border to oppose the growers' use of illegal immigrants as temporary replacement workers during a strike.

This issue of protecting the labor market so that wages are kept high is as relevant today as it was a hundred years ago.

Do a little math. As of March 2010, there were 15 million Americans unemployed, for an unemployment rate of 9.7 percent, according to the federal Bureau of Labor Statistics (BLS). The number of "long-term unemployed" (those unemployed for 27 weeks or more) was 6.5 million. Another 9.1 million Americans were "involuntarily" working part-time, meaning either their hours were cut back or they could not find full-time work. Another 2.3 million Americans had simply given up looking for work and were not even counted among the unemployed, according to the BLS.[5]

So a snapshot of the labor situation in March 2010 shows us that there were more than *32 million* Americans who were unemployed or underemployed.

At the same time, the number of illegal immigrants in the United States quadrupled from 3 million in 1980 to almost 12 million in 2008,[6] no doubt diluting our labor pool. A parallel trend—

not entirely unrelated—shows that the percentage of the private workforce in the United States that was unionized declined from roughly 25 percent in the early 1980s to around 7 percent in 2009.

The way we can deal with the immigration problem is, first, not to treat it as an immigration problem. It is really a problem of the supply and demand of labor or, more accurately, cheap labor. We need to first focus on reducing, if not eliminating, the *demand* for cheap labor. This means going after the businesses that are hiring all the illegal immigrants at poverty-level wages.

So long as employers are willing and able (without severe penalties) to hire illegal workers, people will risk life and limb to grab at the America Dream. When we stop hiring and paying them, most will leave of their own volition over a few years, and the remaining few who are committed to the United States will obtain citizenship through normal channels.

We also need to require that *all* nonrefugee immigrants go through the same process to become American citizens or legal workers in this country (no amnesties, no "guest workers," no "legalizations") regardless of how they got here. And we need to make it clear that while health care is a human right and anyone needing medical service while in the United States will get it, no one has the right to a public education or a job or any government help unless they are here legally.

A common response and criticism to these remedies is this: but if illegal immigrants won't pick our produce or bus our tables, won't our prices go up?

The answer is simple: yes.

But wages would also go up, and even faster than housing, consumer products, and food prices. All working Americans would gladly pay a bit more at the store or restaurant if their paychecks were both significantly higher and more secure.

One problem with implementing these measures is that Democrats and progressives—as well as some labor unions—have taken the bait and begun to look at what they perceive to be ad-

vantages in the growing immigrant population. It's frankly astonishing to hear "progressives" reciting corporatist and conservative
talking points, recycled through "conservative" Democratic politicians, in an effort to pander to the relatively small percentage
of newly legal (mostly through recent amnesties or birth) immigrants. It's equally astonishing to hear unions going along with this
(in the desperate hope of picking up new members) and embracing illegal immigration.

Every nation has an obligation to limit immigration to a
number that will not dilute its workforce but will maintain a stable
middle class—if it wants to have a stable democracy. This has
nothing to do with race, national origin, or language and everything to do with economics.

Other Ways to Tighten the Workforce

Here's another way to tighten up our labor market and thus raise
wages and our standard of living: lower the Social Security retirement age from the current 65–67 to 55 and increase the benefits
to where they were in inflation-adjusted 1960s dollars by raising
them between 10 to 20 percent (so people could actually live, albeit modestly, on Social Security).

The right-wing reaction to this, of course, will be to say that
with fewer people working and more people drawing benefits, it
would bankrupt Social Security and destroy the economy.

But history shows the exact reverse. It would instead eliminate the problem of unemployment in the United States. All those
Boomers retiring would make room in the labor market for all the
recent high school and college graduates, who are now finding it
so hard to get a job.

Thus a tightened labor market would increase wages. And as
wages go up, tax revenues—which are paying for Social Security
(among other things)—would increase.

Additionally, these new-into-the-workforce people can then pay off student loans, buy new houses and cars, and otherwise drive the economy from the bottom up (which is the only way that actually works). This will increase tax revenues even more, further strengthening the Social Security system.

What all of the above measures—cracking down on illegal employers, standardizing citizenship procedures for all nonrefugee applicants, banning any government services for illegal immigrants other than urgent medical care, and lowering the retirement age to 55—will do is ultimately tighten our labor market.

And a tighter labor market will improve wages and once again result in a stable middle class.

Bring Back the Unions

Probably the most visible evidence of a strong middle class—in every nation in the world—is a strong and vibrant union movement.

In Europe's industrial powerhouse Germany, for example, not only are virtually all industries unionized but the law *requires* that half of the members of the boards of directors of every corporation in the country be composed of representatives of the workers via the union. It was one of those little things—like a national health-care system—that Harry Truman made sure got slipped into German law as the nation was being rebuilt from the rubble of World War II. The timing was particularly ironic in that at about that time—1947—the U.S. Congress had been taken over by Republicans, who, over Truman's veto, passed the Taft-Hartley Act that legalized the union-busting for which Reagan became so famous.

Ever since 1947 American labor unions have been fighting an uphill battle, and every loss for organized labor has been a loss for the middle class.

"Supply-side" insanity aside, any real economist can tell you that a nation's economy grows because wages grow, increasing the purchasing power of an economic class that spends most everything its earns.

As wages go up, purchases go up. As purchases go up, demand goes up. As demand goes up, entrepreneurs will notice opportunities to meet it and create new products and start new businesses and then hire people to create the product or service they noticed.

It all begins with increasing wages.

And in America, from the founding of our republic until around 1980—about 200 years—the growth of wages had been on a steady upward trajectory. Wages produce *demand,* and in a supply-and-demand economy such as we have, *supply* is created by *productivity.*

Interestingly, the increase in wages pretty much perfectly tracked the increase in industrial productivity from 1786 until 1980. People earned more, and they bought more (there were hiccups for several of our large wars, but they leveled out as soon as the wars were over). As people bought more, industry became more productive both in efficiency and gross output. Supply and demand were in balance.

Supply-side Insanity

Then, in the 1980s, Art Laffer and Ronald Reagan and David Stockman rolled out an insane economic theory that they called "supply-side economics" (George H. W. Bush called it "voodoo economics"). Basically, it said that demand didn't matter. If there was more stuff for people to buy, that surplus of goods would *create* the demand. And because with supply-side you could create a "new" type of demand—unlike "old-fashioned" demand that comes from wages—then wages didn't matter, either. (This is why Reagan felt just fine, thank you very much, about taking a meat ax to the modern labor movement.)

Thus from the early 1980s until this day, wages of working people in America have been pretty much flat, while supply (productivity) has continued to rise. As the two lines separated, the gap had to be filled with something—and Alan Greenspan had just the thing.

Credit.

The Credit Trap

While American working people's wages have been under relentless attack—with the largest part of that assault being against the unions, which protect wages—working people were encouraged to keep buying more and more. Even after 9/11, George W. Bush knew the drill without dropping a beat when asked what Americans could do to help the nation: "Go shopping" was his instant response.

But with what money?

Alan Greenspan opened up the spigots to credit in the 1980s to fill in that "wage gap," so credit cards that used to be very difficult to get were everywhere. In the late 1990s and the early 2000s, he further opened credit lines to include letting people use their home equity as if their house were an ATM.*

So American working people went from earning and spending to borrowing and spending. We maxed out our credit cards, then wiped out the equity in our homes.

Instead of the extra money from increased supply/productivity going to workers, it could now go to CEOs, who saw their compensation rise from 30:1 in 1980 to 500:1 in 2004. What was left over went to what the *Wall Street Journal* calls the "investor class," and the stock market went from around 1,000 when Reagan was elected to nearly 14,000 in 2008—a massive transfer of wealth from wage earners to investors.

The banksters then made off with whatever else was left, and the working people of America found themselves with nothing

---

*A brilliant book on this is economist Dr. Ravi Batra's *Greenspan's Fraud: How Two Decades of His Policies Have Undermined the Global Economy* (Basingstoke, Hampshire, U.K.: Palgrave Macmillan, 2005).

much more than a corporate-funded Tea Party to attend to express their outrage at the state of things.

Here's where another primary benefit that unions provide to society (and workers) comes in: they supply a countervailing balance to the power of aggregated capital. If money can organize (and it does, in the corporate form), then labor must organize to balance the excesses of unrestrained capital. Unions are democracies; corporations are kingdoms. Within historic monarchies like the United Kingdom and Norway, a strong democratic institution balancing the kingdom (parliament) has produced a positive and sustainable result. We need democracy in the workplace for American business to optimize its competing forces of ownership, management, workers, and community—a democracy that only unions can provide.

Straightening Out the Mess

The solution is to rebalance the power shift that's occurred since 1981 by bringing back the unions. If we rolled back Taft-Hartley—or even went halfway in that direction by passing the Employee Free Choice Act—wages would begin to rise again toward the direction of productivity. This would produce *real* stimulus to the economy (as opposed to the phony stimulus of debt-based spending); and as our economy grows, our tax base grows.

As the tax base grows, we can pay down our debts and actually go back to building things here like schools and hospitals and high-speed rail lines. (There's a simple reason why so much of our nation's infrastructure—including our interstate highway system, which would cost trillions to reproduce—was built during the unionized halcyon days of 1950 to 1980, and so little since then. Back then we had high wages for working people, producing a real and healthy economy, which in turn produced a stable base for property taxes and other infrastructure-funding revenue sources.)

So to bring back a strong middle class, we need to bring back the unions while we're cleaning up our labor surplus with comprehensive immigration reform.

This is particularly important now because without a middle class, any democracy is doomed. And without labor's having power in relative balance to capital/management—through control of labor availability—no middle class *can* emerge. America's early labor leaders did not die to increase the labor pool for the robber barons or the Walton family; they died fighting to give control of it to the workers of their era and in the hopes that we would continue to hold it—and to inspire other nations with the same idea of democracy and a stable middle class.

This is, after all, the middle-class American Dream. And think how much better this hemisphere would be if Central and South Americans were motivated to stay in their own nations (because no employer in the United States would dare hire them illegally) and fight *there* for a Mexican Dream and a Salvadoran Dream and a Guatemalan Dream, and so on. It means a better quality of life for everyone, rather than our lax immigrant-employment enforcements providing a political and social safety valve for repressive or regressive conservative Central and South American nations.

This is the historic progressive vision for *all* of the Americas.

CHAPTER 10

Wal-Mart Is *Not* a Person

> *The peculiar evil of silencing the expression of an opinion*
> *is that it is robbing the human race; posterity as well as the*
> *existing generation; those who dissent from the opinion,*
> *still more than those who hold it. If the opinion is right,*
> *they are deprived of the opportunity of exchanging error for*
> *truth: if wrong, they lose, what is almost as great a benefit,*
> *the clearer perception and livelier impression of truth,*
> *produced by its collision with error.*
>
> —John Stuart Mill

IN 2003, AFTER MY BOOK *UNEQUAL PROTECTION* WAS FIRST PUB-lished, I gave a talk at one of the larger law schools in Vermont. Around 300 people showed up, mostly students, with a few dozen faculty and some local lawyers. I started by asking, "Please raise your hand if you *know* that in 1886, in the *Santa Clara County v. Southern Pacific Railroad* case, the Supreme Court ruled that corporations are persons and therefore entitled to rights under the Constitution and the Bill of Rights."

Almost everyone in the room raised their hand, and the few who didn't probably were new enough to the law that they hadn't gotten to study that case yet. Nobody questioned the basic premise of the statement.

And all of them were wrong.

We the People are the first three words of the Preamble to the Constitution; and from its adoption until the Robber Baron Era in the late nineteenth century, *people* meant human beings. In the 1886 *Santa Clara* case, however, the court reporter of the Supreme Court proclaimed in a "headnote"—a summary or statement added at the top of the court decision, which is separate from the decision and has no legal force whatsoever—that the word *person* in law and, particularly, in the Constitution, meant both humans *and* corporations.

Thus began in a big way (it actually started a half century earlier in a much smaller way with a case involving Dartmouth University) the corruption of American democracy and the shift, over the 125 years since then, to our modern corporate oligarchy.

Most recently, in a January 2010 ruling in *Citizens United v. Federal Election Commission,* the Supreme Court, under Chief Justice John G. Roberts, took the radical step of overturning more than a hundred years of laws passed by elected legislatures and signed by elected presidents and declared that not only are corporations "persons" but that they have constitutional rights such as the First Amendment right to free speech.

This decision is clear evidence of how far we have drifted away as a nation from our foundational principles and values. Particularly since the presidency of Ronald Reagan, over the past three decades our country and its democratic ideals have been hijacked by what Joseph Pulitzer a hundred years ago famously called "predatory plutocracy."

The *Citizens United* decision, which empowers and elevates corporations above citizens, is not just a symbolic but a *real* threat to our democracy, and only the will of We the People, exercised through a constitutional amendment to deny personhood to corporations, can slay the dragon the Court has unleashed.

The "Disadvantaged" Corporation

In 2008 a right-wing group named *Citizens United* put together a 90-minute "documentary," a flat-out hit-job on Hillary Clinton (then a senator and presidential aspirant) and wanted to run commercials promoting it on TV stations in strategic states. The Federal Election Commission (FEC) ruled that the movie and the television advertisements promoting it were really "campaign ads" and stopped them from airing because they violated McCain-Feingold (aka the Bipartisan Campaign Reform Act of 2002), which bars "independent expenditures" by corporations, unions, or other organizations 30 days before a primary election or 60 days before a general election. (Direct corporate contributions to campaigns of candidates have been banned repeatedly and in various ways since 1907, when Teddy Roosevelt pushed through the Tillman Act, which made it a felony for a corporation to give money to a politician for federal office; in 1947 the Taft-Hartley Act extended this ban to unions.)

McCain-Feingold was a good bipartisan achievement by conservative senator John McCain and liberal senator Russ Feingold to limit the ability of corporations to interfere around the edges of campaigns. The law required the "I'm John McCain and I approve this message" disclaimer and limited the amount of money that could be spent on any federal politician's behalf in campaign advertising. It also limited the ability of multimillionaires to finance their own elections.

But the law offended the members of the economic elite in this country who call themselves "conservatives" and believe that they should be able to spend vast amounts of money to influence electoral and legislative outcomes.

The Conservative Worldview

In part, this belief is derived from a more fundamental—and insidious—belief that political power in the hands of average working people is dangerous and destabilizing to America; this is the source of the antipathy of such conservatives to both democracy and labor unions. They believe in "original sin"—that we're all essentially evil and corruptible (because we came out of the womb of a woman, who was heir to Eve's apple-eating)—and therefore it's necessary for a noble, well-educated, and wealthy (male) elite, working behind the scenes, to make the rules for and run our society.

Among the chief proponents of this Bible-based view of the errancy of average working people are the five right-wing members of the current U.S. Supreme Court—John Roberts, Samuel Alito, Clarence Thomas, Antonin Scalia, and Anthony Kennedy—who have consistently worked to make America more hierarchical, only with a small, wealthy "conservative/corporate" elite in charge instead of a divinely ordained Pope.

And even though the *Citizens United* case—which landed in the Supreme Court's lap after the federal court in Washington, D.C., ruled in favor of the FEC ban—was only about a small slice of the McCain-Feingold law, the Republican Five used it as an opportunity to make a monumental change to constitutionally empower corporations and undo a century of legal precedents.

After listening to oral arguments in early 2009, the Roberts Court chose to ignore those arguments and the originally narrow pleadings in the case, expanded the scope of the case, and scheduled hearings for September of that year, asking that the breadth of the arguments include reexamining the rationales for Congress to have *any* power to regulate corporate "free speech."

In this they were going along with a request from Theodore B. "Ted" Olson, the solicitor general under George W. Bush, and would now go back to reexamine and perhaps overturn the Court's own precedent in the *Austin v. Michigan Chamber of Commerce* case of 1990. In that case the Court held that it was constitutional for Congress to place limits on corporate political activities; and in a 2003 case, the Court (before the additions of Alito and Roberts) had already upheld McCain-Feingold as constitutional.[1]

Thus, on January 21, 2010, in a 5-to-4 decision, the Supreme Court ruled in the *Citizens United* case that it is unconstitutional for Congress to approve, or the president to sign into law, most restrictions on the "right" of a corporate "person" to heavily influence political campaigns so long as they don't directly donate to the politicians' campaign or party.

The majority decision, written by Justice Kennedy at the direction of Chief Justice Roberts, explicitly states that the government has virtually no right to limit corporate power when it comes to corporate "free speech."[2]

Kennedy began this line of reasoning by positing, "Premised on mistrust of governmental power, the First Amendment stands against attempts to disfavor certain subjects or viewpoints."

It sounds reasonable. He even noted, sounding almost like Martin Luther King Jr. or John F. Kennedy, that:

> By taking the right to speak from some and giving it to others, the Government deprives the disadvantaged person or class of the right to use speech to strive to establish worth, standing, and respect for the speaker's voice. The Government may not by these means deprive the public of the right and privilege to determine for itself what speech and speakers are worthy of consideration.

But who is that "disadvantaged person or class" of whom Kennedy was speaking? His answer is quite blunt (the parts in single quotation marks are where he is quoting from previous Supreme Court decisions): "The Court has recognized that First Amendment protection extends to corporations.... Under that rationale of these precedents, political speech does not lose First Amendment protection 'simply because its source is a corporation.'"

Two sentences later he nails it home: "The Court has thus rejected the argument that political speech of corporations or other associations should be treated differently under the First Amendment simply because such associations are not 'natural persons.'" (Historically, *natural persons* has been the term for humans under both British common law and American constitutional law; corporations, churches, and governments are referred to as *artificial persons.*)

Bemoaning how badly corporations and their trade associations (like the U.S. Chamber of Commerce, the nation's leading front-group player in both national and local politics for decades and the number one lobbyist in terms of spending) had been treated by the Congress of the United States for more than a hundred years, Kennedy stuck up for the "disadvantaged" corporate "persons" the Roberts Court was seeking to protect:

> The censorship we now confront is vast in its reach. The Government has "muffled the voices that best represent the most significant segments of the economy." And "the electorate has been deprived of information, knowledge, and opinion vital to its function." By suppressing the speech of manifold corporations, both for-profit and non-profit, the Government prevents their voices and viewpoints from reaching the public and advising voters on which persons or entities are hostile to their interests.

By reinterpreting the Fourteenth Amendment, which says that no "person" (the amendment's authors didn't add the word *natural* because it was written to free the slaves after the Civil War, so they figured *person* was sufficient) shall be denied equal protection under the law, the Roberts Court turned American democracy inside out. "We the People" now explicitly means "We the Citizens, Corporations, and Churches" with a few of the richest humans who run them thrown in.

Such a view is antithetical to how the Framers of our Constitution viewed corporations.

A Historical Perspective

The Founders of this nation were so wary of corporate power that when the British Parliament voted to give a massive tax break—through the Tea Act of 1773—to the East India Company on thousands of tons of tea it had in stock so that the company could wipe out its small, entrepreneurial colonial competitors, the colonists staged the Boston Tea Party.

This act of vandalism against the world's largest transnational corporation, destroying more than a million dollars' worth (in today's money) of corporate property, led the British to pass the Boston Ports Act of 1774, which declared the Port of Boston closed to commerce until the city paid back the East India Company for its spoiled tea. It was an economic embargo like we declared against Cuba, Iraq, and Iran, and it led the colonists straight into open rebellion and the Revolutionary War.

Thus the Framers of our Constitution intentionally chose not to even use the word *corporation* in that document, as they wanted business entities and churches to be legally established at the state level, where local governments could keep an eye on them.

Throughout most of the first 100 years of our nation, corporations were severely restricted so that they could not gain too much power or wealth. It was illegal for a corporation to buy or own stock in another corporation, to engage in more than one type of business, to participate in politics, and to even exist for more than 40 years (so that the corporate form couldn't be used by wealthy and powerful families to amass great wealth in an intergenerational way and avoid paying an estate tax).

All of that came to an end during the "chartermongering" era of the 1890s when, after Ohio prepared to charge John D. Rockefeller with antitrust and other violations of the corporate laws of that state, he challenged other states to broaden and loosen their laws regarding corporate charters. A competition broke out among, primarily, Connecticut, New Jersey, New York, and Delaware, which Delaware ultimately won by enacting laws that were the most corporate-friendly in the nation. This is the reason why today more than half of the NYSE-listed companies are Delaware corporations.

In addition, the largest corporations of the era—the railroads—began a relentless campaign in the 1870s that reached its zenith in 1886, claiming that as "corporate persons" they should have "rights" under the Bill of Rights in the Constitution. That zenith was the *Santa Clara County v. Southern Pacific Railroad* case, where the Supreme Court did *not* rule that corporations are persons, but the court reporter claimed it had, establishing language that was cited repeatedly in subsequent Court decisions ratifying this newly found "corporate personhood" doctrine and cementing it into law.*

A Patriotic Dissent

When the Republican Five on the Supreme Court ruled in the *Citizens United* case and handed to corporations nearly full human rights of free speech, it didn't come out of the blue. Although no bill in Congress from the time of George Washington to Barack Obama had declared that corporations should have these "human rights" (to the contrary, multiple laws had said the opposite), and no president had ever spoken in favor of corporate human rights, the five men in the majority on the Supreme Court took it upon themselves to hand our country over to the tender mercies of the world's largest transnational corporations.

---

*The historical facts of Santa Clara County v. Southern Pacific Railroad are explored in depth in Thom Hartmann, *Unequal Protection: How Corporations Became "People"—and How You Can Fight Back,* 2nd ed. (San Francisco: Berrett-Koehler, 2010).

The Court's Minority Pushes Back

This didn't sit well with the other four members of the Supreme Court.

Justice John Paul Stevens, with the concurrence of Justices Ruth Bader Ginsburg, Stephen Breyer, and Sonia Sotomayor, wrote the dissenting opinion in the *Citizens United* case.

Calling the decision "misguided" in the first paragraph of the 90-page dissent, Stevens (and his colleagues) pointed out that the Court majority had just effectively handed our country over to any foreign interest willing to incorporate here and spend money on political TV ads.

> If taken seriously, our colleagues' assumption that the identity of a speaker has no relevance to the Government's ability to regulate political speech would lead to some remarkable conclusions. Such an assumption would have accorded the propaganda broadcasts to our troops by "Tokyo Rose" during World War II the same protection as speech by Allied commanders. More pertinently, it would appear to afford the same protection to multinational corporations controlled by foreigners as to individual Americans: To do otherwise, after all, could "'enhance the relative voice'" of some (i.e., humans) over others (i.e., corporations).

In the same paragraph, Stevens further points out the absurdity of granting corporations what are essentially citizenship rights under the Constitution, suggesting that perhaps the next Court decision will be to give corporations the right to vote: "Under the majority's view, I suppose it may be a First Amendment problem that corporations are not permitted to vote, given that voting is, among other things, a form of speech."

Quoting earlier Supreme Court cases and the Founders, Stevens wrote: "The word 'soulless' constantly recurs in debates over corporations...Corporations, it was feared, could concentrate the worst urges of whole groups of men." Thomas Jefferson famously fretted that corporations would subvert the republic.

And, Stevens reasoned, the Founders could not have possibly meant to confer First Amendment rights on corporations when they adopted the Constitution in 1787 and proposed the Bill of Rights in 1789 because, "All general business corporation statutes appear to date from well after 1800":

> The Framers thus took it as a given that corporations could be comprehensively regulated in the service of the public welfare. Unlike our colleagues, they had little trouble distinguishing corporations from human beings, and when they constitutionalized the right to free speech in the First Amendment, it was the free speech of individual Americans they had in mind.

To make his point, Stevens even quoted Chief Justice John Marshall, who served from his appointment by President John Adams in 1800 until 1835, making him one of America's longest-serving chief justices. Sometimes referred to as the "father of the Supreme Court," Marshall had written in an early-nineteenth-century decision some text Stevens quoted into his *Citizen's United* dissent: "A corporation is an artificial being, invisible, intangible, and existing only in contemplation of law. Being a mere creature of law, it posses only those properties which the charter of its creation confers upon it."

Stevens's dissent called out Roberts, Alito, Scalia, Thomas, and Kennedy for their behavior in the *Citizen's United* ruling, which he said was "the height of recklessness to dismiss Congress' years of bipartisan deliberation and its reasoned judgment...":

> The fact that corporations are different from human beings might seem to need no elaboration, except that the majority opinion almost completely elides it....Unlike natural persons, corporations have "limited liability" for their owners and managers, "perpetual life," separation of ownership and control, "and favorable treatment of the accumulation of assets...that

enhance their ability to attract capital and to deploy their resources in ways that maximize the return on their shareholders'
investments." Unlike voters in U.S. elections, corporations may
be foreign controlled.

Noting that "they inescapably structure the life of every citizen," Stevens continued:

> It might be added that corporations have no consciences, no
> beliefs, no feelings, no thoughts, no desires. Corporations help
> structure and facilitate the activities of human beings, to be sure,
> and their "personhood" often serves as a useful legal fiction. But
> they are not themselves members of "We the People" by whom
> and for whom our Constitution was established.

In this very eloquent and pointed dissent, Stevens even
waxed philosophical, asking a series of questions for which there
couldn't possible be any clear or obvious answers if the Court were
to maintain the "logic" of its *Citizens United* ruling:

> It is an interesting question "who" is even speaking when a
> business corporation places an advertisement that endorses or
> attacks a particular candidate. Presumably it is not the custom-
> ers or employees, who typically have no say in such matters. It
> cannot realistically be said to be the shareholders, who tend to
> be far removed from the day-to-day decisions of the firm and
> whose political preferences may be opaque to management.
> Perhaps the officers or directors of the corporation have the best
> claim to be the ones speaking, except their fiduciary duties gen-
> erally prohibit them from using corporate funds for personal
> ends. Some individuals associated with the corporation must
> make the decision to place the ad, but the idea that these indi-
> viduals are thereby fostering their self-expression or cultivating
> their critical faculties is fanciful.

The dissenting justices argued that the majority's ruling
wasn't merely wrong, both in a contemporary and a historical
sense, but that it was *dangerous.* The dissent was explicit, clear,

and shocking in how bluntly the three most senior members of the Court (along with the newbie, Sotomayor) called out their colleagues, two of whom (Roberts and Alito) had been just recently appointed by George W. Bush.

The dissenters noted that it was their five colleagues (and their friends in high places) who were clamoring for corporations to have personhood and free-speech rights, *not* the American people who were the "listeners" of such speech: "It is only certain Members of this Court, not the listeners themselves, who have agitated for more corporate electioneering."

They continued, noting that corporate interests are inherently different from the public (and human) interests:*

> [The] *Austin* [Supreme Court decision that upheld McCain/Feingold in 2003] recognized that there are substantial reasons why a legislature might conclude that unregulated general treasury expenditures will give corporations "unfair influence" in the electoral process, and distort public debate in ways that undermine rather than advance the interests of listeners. The legal structure of corporations allows them to amass and deploy financial resources on a scale few natural persons can match. The structure of a business corporation, furthermore, draws a line between the corporation's economic interests and the political preferences of the individuals associated with the corporation; the corporation must engage the electoral process with the aim "to enhance the profitability of the company, no matter how persuasive the arguments for a broader or conflicting set of priorities."

By having free-speech rights equal with people, Stevens argued, corporations will actually harm the "competition among

---

*Again, the words in quotation marks are where, in the dissent, the justices themselves are quoting from previous Supreme Court rulings. I've removed all the reference citations, as they make it hard to read; anybody wanting to dive deeper into this 90-page dissent can read it online at www.supreme court.gov/opinions/09pdf/08-205.pdf.

ideas" that the Framers envisioned when they wrote the First Amendment:

> "[A] corporation…should have as its objective the conduct of business activities with a view to enhancing corporate profit and shareholder gain." In a state election…the interests of nonresident corporations may be fundamentally adverse to the interests of local voters. Consequently, when corporations grab up the prime broadcasting slots on the eve of an election, they can flood the market with advocacy that bears little or no correlation to the ideas of natural persons or to any broader notion of the public good. The opinions of real people may be marginalized.

Moreover, just the fact that corporations can participate on an unlimited basis as actors in the political process will, inevitably, cause average working Americans—the 99 percent who make less than $300,000 a year—to conclude that their "democracy" is now rigged.

The result will be that more and more people will simply stop participating in politics (it's interesting to note how many politicians announced within weeks of this decision that they would not run for reelection), stop being informed about politics, and stop voting. Our democracy will wither and could even die.

> When citizens turn on their televisions and radios before an election and hear only corporate electioneering, they may lose faith in their capacity, as citizens, to influence public policy. A Government captured by corporate interests, they may come to believe, will be neither responsive to their needs nor willing to give their views a fair hearing.

> The predictable result is cynicism and disenchantment: an increased perception that large spenders "call the tune" and a reduced "willingness of voters to take part in democratic governance."

And even if humans were willing to try to take on corporations (maybe a billionaire or two with good ethics would run for office?), virtually every single person who tries to run for office will have to dance to the corporate tune or risk being totally destroyed by the huge and now-unlimited amounts of cash that corporations can rain down on our heads.

> The majority's unwillingness to distinguish between corporations and humans similarly blinds it to the possibility that corporations' "war chests" and their special "advantages" in the legal realm may translate into special advantages in the market for legislation.

Scalia Is Offended

Horrified by the blunt language of the dissent and of being called "misguided," "dangerous," and "reckless" by his colleagues, Justice Scalia wrote a short concurring opinion in an attempt to once more speak up for the "disadvantaged" corporations:

> Despite the corporation-hating quotations the dissent has dredged up, it is far from clear that by the end of the 18th century corporations were despised. If so, how came there to be so many of them?…Indeed, to exclude or impede corporate speech is to muzzle the principal agents of the modern free economy. We should celebrate rather than condemn the addition of this [corporate] speech to the public debate.

Justice Roberts offered his own short concurring opinion, in self-defense, saying that for "our democracy" to work, the voices in the public arena shouldn't just be a human on a soapbox but *must* include massive transnational corporations:

> First Amendment rights could be confined to individuals, subverting the vibrant public discourse that is at the foundation of our democracy.

> The Court properly rejects that theory, and I join its opinion in full. The first Amendment protects more than just the individual on a soapbox and the lonely pamphleteer.

In other words, if a single corporation spends $700 million in television advertising to tell you that, for example, Senator Bernie Sanders is a "bad person" because he sponsored legislation that limits its profitability, and Sanders can raise only $3 million to defend himself with a few local TV spots, that's just the reality of "the vibrant public discourse that is at the foundation of our democracy."

The Decision and the Damage Done

There is no better evidence of the harm that the *Citizens United* decision poses to our democracy than to see the immediate reaction from the corporations—or, more accurately, the persons who run the corporations.

Two weeks after the decision, a headline in the *New York Times* said: "In a Message to Democrats, Wall St. Sends Cash to G.O.P." The article quoted banking industry sources (who now knew that they could use their considerable financial power politically) as saying that they were experiencing "buyer's remorse" over having given Obama and the Democrats $89 million in 2008: "Republicans are rushing to capitalize on what they call Wall Street's 'buyer's remorse' with the Democrats. And industry executives and lobbyists are warning Democrats that if Mr. Obama keeps attacking Wall Street 'fat cats,' they may fight back by withholding their cash."[3]

The article quoted several banking sources as saying they were outraged that the president had criticized their industry for the financial meltdown of 2008 or their big bonuses. It wrapped up with a quote from John Cornyn, the senator from Texas tasked with raising money for the National Republican Senatorial Committee, noting that he was now making regular visits to Wall Street in New York City. Speaking of the Democrats who dared challenge the banksters, he crowed: "I just don't know how long you can expect people to contribute money to a political party whose main plank of their platform is to punish you."

It was a loud shot across Obama's bow, and within two weeks the president had changed his tune on a wide variety of initiatives, ranging from taxes on the wealthy to backing away from truly strong regulations on the banking, insurance, and pharmaceutical industries and instead embracing more-cosmetic "reforms."

The fact is that about $5 billion was spent in *all* the political campaigns from coast to coast in the elections of 2008, a bit less than $2 billion of that on the presidential race. Compare that with January 2010, when a small cadre of senior executives and employees of the nation's top banks on Wall Street split up among themselves more than $145 billion in *personal bonus* money.

If those few thousand people had decided to take just 3 percent of their bonus and redirect it into a political campaign, no politician in America could stand against them. And now none do. And that's just the banksters! Profits in the tens and hundreds of billions of dollars were reported in 2009 by the oil, pharmaceutical, insurance, agriculture, and retailing industries—all now considering how to use a small part of their profits to influence political races.

While WellPoint's Anthem Blue Cross division was raising insurance rates in California by up to 36 percent, the company declared a quarterly profit of well over $2 billion. And the six largest oil companies were making more than a billion dollars in *profits* per week. Even the smallest coalition, funneling their money through the U.S. Chamber of Commerce, now has the ability to promote or destroy any politician.

There are now no limits to what corporations (or rich individuals using a corporation as a front) can spend to influence elections or ballot measures. Every member of Congress will now know before he or she votes in favor of any legislation that is opposed by a particular industry, or votes against a bill that is favored by that industry, that it will have consequences come reelection time.

Anyone concerned with the integrity of the political system should note that this decision affects the legitimacy of elections not only of the legislative and executive branches but also of judges. As Bill Moyers and Michael Winship wrote in the *Huffington Post* in February 2010,[4]

> Ninety-eight percent of all the lawsuits in this country take place in the state courts. In 39 states, judges have to run for election— that's more than 80 percent of the state judges in America.

> The *Citizens United* decision made those judges who are elected even more susceptible to the corrupting influence of cash, for many of their decisions in civil cases directly affect corporate America, and a significant amount of the money judges raise for their campaigns comes from lobbyists and lawyers.

Those inclined to underestimate the influence of cash on judicial elections should be reminded of some basic facts that Moyers and Winship provided:

> During the 1990s, candidates for high court judgeships in states around the country and the parties that supported them raised $85 million...for their campaigns. Since the year 2000, the numbers have more than doubled to over $200 million.

> The nine justices currently serving on the Texas Supreme Court have raised nearly $12 million in campaign contributions. The race for a seat on the Pennsylvania Supreme Court last year was the most expensive judicial race in the country, with more than four and a half million dollars spent by the Democrats and Republicans. With the Supreme Court's *Citizens United* decision, corporate money's muscle got a big hypodermic needle full of steroids.

This decision was a naked handoff of raw political power to corporate forces by five unelected judges; and as we saw earlier, the other four members of the Court said so in the plainest and most blunt terms.

Indeed, the First Amendment now protects the "free speech" rights of the presidents of Russia and China and Iran to form corporations in the United States and pour millions of dollars toward supporting or defeating members of Congress or presidential aspirants who favor trade policies or a foreign policy that suits their interests.

This decision also protects the "right" of the largest polluting corporations on earth to politically destroy any politician who wants to give any more authority to the Environmental Protection Agency or to elevate to elected status any politician who is willing to dismantle the EPA.

This Supreme Court decision has vested power in already-powerful corporations that they never had before: to directly affect the outcome of elections for public office and of ballot measures.

So what's to be done?

Such a radical decision requires an equally radical response that must be both far-reaching and permanent.

Move to Amend

There are only three ways to undo a bad Supreme Court decision. All three have been used at various times.

The first is to wait until the composition of the Court changes —one or more of the bad judges retires or dies and is replaced by others more competent. (It's worth noting that even former Justice Sandra Day O'Connor, a Ronald Reagan appointee and longtime Republican activist, condemned the *Citizens United* ruling.) Then the Court takes on a case that involves the same issues and, like with *Brown v. Board of Education* and *Roe v. Wade,* pushes the Court forward in time.

The second is for the American people, the president, and Congress to understand the horror of the consequences of such a decision and break with the Court.

Arguably, this happened with the *Dred Scott v. Sanford* decision in 1857, which ruled that black *persons* were actually *property* and thus led us directly into the Civil War. That Supreme Court decision led to Abraham Lincoln's Emancipation Proclamation and the passage of legislation clarifying the rights of African Americans, although it ultimately took a war and the passage of the 13th, 14th, and 15th Amendments to purge slavery from our laws and our Constitution.

Ironically, the *Citizens United* case is the mirror of *Dred Scott* in that it ruled that a *property*—a corporation—is now a *person*.

The third way to undo—or supersede—a Supreme Court decision is to amend the Constitution itself so that the Court can no longer play with the semantics of ambiguous or broadly worded language. We did this, for example, to both institute and then repeal the prohibition, manufacture, and sale of alcohol.

The constitutional amendment route seems the most practical and long lasting, even though it may be the most challenging.

More than 29,000 amendments to our Constitution have been put forth in Congress since the founding of our republic, and only 27 have passed the hurdle of approval by two-thirds of the members of Congress and three-fourths of the states. Nonetheless, successful amendments are driven by a widespread sense that the change is absolutely essential for the good of the nation.

An example of this is the Twenty-sixth Amendment to drop the voting age from 21 to 18. It was largely brought about by the rage and the impotence that young people felt in America during the Vietnam War era (as expressed in the song "Eve of Destruction": "You're old enough to kill, but not for votin'…"). The need for young people to participate in a political process that could lead them to war was so clear that the Twenty-sixth Amendment passed the

Senate in March 1971 and was completely ratified by the states on July 1, 1971.

As Americans see our politicians repeatedly being corrupted by corporate influence—from health care to banking to labor standards to the environment—and the middle class continues to collapse as a result, this may well be one of those moments in time when an amendment can make it through the Congress and the states in a relatively short time.

Several proposals are on the table, but I particularly recommend the models put forth by Jeff Milchen and David Cobb. Milchen, who founded ReclaimDemocracy.org, is one of the leading resources on the issue of corporate personhood; and Cobb's Web site, www.MoveToAmend.org, incorporates Jeff's proposed constitutional amendment as well as other options. Milchen's proposed amendment, more explicit than simply inserting the word *natural* before the word *person* in the Fourteenth Amendment, could seriously begin the process of returning the United States to a democratic republic that is once again responsive and responsible to its citizens instead of its most powerful corporations. The proposed amendment reads as follows:

> **Section 1.** The U.S. Constitution protects only the rights of living human beings.
>
> **Section 2.** Corporations and other institutions granted the privilege to exist shall be subordinate to any and all laws enacted by citizens and their elected governments.
>
> **Section 3.** Corporations and other for-profit institutions are prohibited from attempting to influence the outcome of elections, legislation or government policy through the use of aggregate resources or by rewarding or repaying employees or directors to exert such influence.
>
> **Section 4.** Congress shall have power to implement this article by appropriate legislation.

Other variations on this amendment, some simpler and some more complex, can be found at www.MoveToAmend.org.

The elegance of explicitly denying constitutional rights to anything except "living human beings" is that it will not only roll back *Citizens United* but also allow future legislatures to challenge corporate claims to "rights" of privacy (Fourth Amendment), protection from self-incrimination (Fifth Amendment), and the power to force themselves on communities that don't want them because to do otherwise is "discrimination" (Fourteenth Amendment).

We must be very careful that any amendment put forth isn't just limited to giving Congress the power to regulate campaign spending; to do so would leave a wide swath of other Bill of Rights powers in the hands of corporations. Instead, an amendment must explicitly overturn the headnote to the 1886 *Santa Clara* decision that asserted that corporations are the same as natural persons in terms of constitutional protections.

By doing this we can begin the transition back from a corporate oligarchic state to the constitutionally limited representative democratic republic our Founders envisioned.

Even before the *Citizens United* case blew open the doors to a corporate takeover of American politics, the corrosive influence of corporations having "rights" was already evident. Now corporate influence in our politics can completely dominate and determine the outcome of elections—unless and until We the People once again assert our right to do what's best for the common good and, through the mechanism of a constitutional amendment, relegate corporations to their rightful place—as legal fictions and not natural persons.

CHAPTER 11

In the Shadow
of the Dragon

*The motivating force of the theory of a democratic
way of life is still a belief that as individuals we live
cooperatively, and, to the best of our ability, serve
the community in which we live, and that our own
success, to be real, must contribute.*

—Eleanor Roosevelt

THERE WAS A DRAGON HERE HUNDREDS OF YEARS AGO, HERE IN
the Basque country in northern Spain, a place steeped in tradition,
a hilly expanse between the mountains and the sea. Local lore has
it that the Basque language, the only European one with no known
root language, is a remnant from the time of Atlantis, which may
have vanished into the Atlantic Ocean not far from here eons ago.

Standing on a hillside overlooking an early autumn valley,
Louise and I were amazed by the simple beauty of the mountain
of the dragon, its gray and balding peak towering above the town
like an ancient ziggurat. This is Mondragon, a small town named
after the dragon of the mountain, the dragon probably being, a
local resident told us, a particularly brutal lord or local king who
exercised the Rite of the First Night, a dreaded ritual when fair
maidens were whisked away on their wedding night.

The Rite of the First Night was said to have been common
across Europe throughout the Dark and Middle Ages, although

it was probably far less common than modern folklore suggests. When a young woman was married, she was required to spend the night of her wedding with—and lose her virginity to—the local lord or king.

Oddly enough, all across Europe one still finds remote communities where most of the people have similar large noses or red hair or big ears and so on—all descendants of some ancient lord who fathered the first children of innumerable families. European society was patriarchal and hierarchal, and because the king lived in distant Toledo, his defilement role was filled by the local lord. The sheer horror of his men coming to take away the new bride became the legend of the dragon.

Now here is the ultimate irony: right here in this valley, in the shadow of the dragon, has grown a business enterprise that—in virtually every way imaginable—is the antithesis of a dragon.

And for all of us in the United States, this business enterprise represents a model that can be transformative and sow the seeds of a new kind of business entity that is, at its heart, more equitable, more fair, and more just—and therefore more truly *American*—than the predatory multinational corporations that are now typical of twenty-first-century America.

Cooperation and Corporation

The Mondragon Cooperative is neither hierarchical nor patriarchal. There's no king or lord. The corporation is owned by its employees. The most highly paid person earns less than six times the most poorly paid person. Decisions are made by workers on the front lines and then communicated up to the "managers" for implementation.

And this is no flaky, hippy-dippy communelike experiment. It is the world's largest federation of cooperatives, employing more than 90,000 people in more than 250 companies that focus on four areas: retail, finance, industry, and knowledge. In 2008, Mondragon's revenue was €16.8 billion ($24.2 billion). All—every last euro cent—of the profits are distributed in one of three ways: reinvested in the business, given to worthy local charities, or paid as dividends to Mondragon's worker-owners.

What Mondragon has shown, by its sheer size, scope, and success, is a new economic model that avoids the pitfalls of both modern capitalism and old-fashioned communism.

"Capitalism" has its deficiencies, whether institutions are for-profit (think Goldman Sachs, where stocks are sold to investors or the public) or not-for-profit (think Red Cross, where the CEO earns $500,000 per year and the "stock" is controlled by a board of directors).

Similarly, "communism" has its problems because the state owns the business, employees are simply agents of the state, and nothing works because nobody is accountable to anybody and there's no incentive to do better.

Most importantly, both capitalism and communism are top-down hierarchies that stifle human ingenuity.

But Mondragon is the world's largest example of a third way: worker-owned cooperatives that foster enterprise as well as equity. Unlike the top-down nature of capitalism and communism, Mondragon has flipped that pyramid upside down.

That flipping is apparent when one visits any of the Mondragon businesses. Louise and I were on the factory floor of an absolutely spotless washing-machine manufacturing facility of the Mondragon Cooperative in 2009 when we witnessed the true cooperative nature of the enterprise. Like all Mondragon businesses, this state-of-the-art industrial facility, converting sheets of raw metal into finished washing machines for sale all around the world, is run by its employees.

As we stood watching, a group of about a dozen workers assembled electronics on a U-shaped assembly line. A "manager" walked up and asked for everyone's attention. Our translator shared with us the essence of the conversation: next Thursday there was going to be a schedule change, the result of some local event.

At first it sounded like a typical manager telling his employees what was what. "Thursday our systems will change, and we'll have to produce a different number of units," he said. The workers nodded.

Then came the bombshell: "How do you all think we should do this?" he asked.

A conversation ensued, and it dawned on me that the workers were not arguing or fighting or complaining; they were offering concrete suggestions. With each suggestion others would point out its strengths or weakness or offer their own.

The "manager" was facilitating the conversation and taking notes. Within 10 minutes some sort of a consensus was achieved, and the workers told the "manager" how they'd handle Thursday's change. He thanked them and left, his job now to communicate up to the cooperative's administrators how the assembly line would adjust itself to Thursday's changes.

This was about as far from the Rite of the First Night as it's possible to imagine. In Mondragon, in the shadow of the ancient—and now dead—dragon, the descendents of the serfs have taken charge. The result is one of the most successful—and equitable—business models in the world.

And it's not just the business pyramid that has been upended; there's a sociocultural element at Mondragon that is just as transformational to its local cultures as is the idea of workers owning and running their own businesses.

Mondragon University was the first institution started here by Don José Maria Arizmendiarrieta, the priest who began in the 1940s what has now grown to become the worldwide Mondragon organization. Investing in education—building knowledge—is like building a factory. Through Mondragon University they're investing in humans just as much as the factories are investing in the business infrastructure of the towns where Mondragon works.

That investment in educating and training students at a university with strong links to the cooperatives is evident in the fact that almost all students find work within weeks of graduation. Mondragon's practice of placing people over profits clearly produces results that benefit all.

Bringing the Lesson Home

Somehow Americans have lost sight of this. We see no benefit in any investment that does not produce profit for the owners, whether the owners are the distant stockholders or the investors or the top executives. Such an attitude not only devalues workers but also fails to recognize the importance of investing in public education, which is particularly tragic given what a difference education can make in social mobility.

The lessons are right before us and easily measurable.

In 1979 the United States was one of the most socially mobile nations in the world, but Reaganomics changed all that. Today the economic class you're born into is the single-most influential factor in determining the economic class in which you'll die. We are the most socially rigid society in the world, having just recently surpassed the royalty-bound United Kingdom.

Similarly, when Ronald Reagan took office in 1981, the income-tax rate for millionaires was 74 percent, which helped keep the average ratio of the lowest-paid worker in a company to its CEO at around 1:30.

Since Reagan cut that tax rate down to near 30 percent, and George W. Bush dropped the top income tax rate for capitalists— people who make their money investing money, who "earn their living" sitting around the pool waiting for the dividend check to arrive—to 15 percent, the ratio is now closer to 1:600; and among many of the Fortune 500 companies, it can be more than 1:5,000.

We've gone from about 25 percent of the workforce being unionized when Reagan took office to about 7 percent of the workforce today. Workers are so terrified of losing their jobs that sexual harassment claims have exploded, and most workers don't even dare report it.

The new Rite of the First Night perpetrators are senior corporate managers and CEOs.

The antidote is to spawn Mondragon Cooperatives of our own.

Time to Think Big

In America we generally know nonprofits and cooperatives to be small, modest operations that are fueled mainly by the passion and the commitment of a core group of dedicated believers, including volunteers or underpaid staff.

That public-service mission is true of nonprofits in general. (Of course, there's been an explosion of sham nonprofits in the USA over the past few decades; for-profit companies have moved to nonprofit status to take advantage of tax exemptions and lower postage rates and then pay their CEOs huge salaries. But that's another rant.)

About two decades ago, Louise and I moved to Vermont. Just down the block from our house was the Hunger Mountain Cooperative, a member-owned health-food store and grocery. As members, Louise and I got an annual distribution check (usually around $100), representing our share of the "profits" of the co-op; and if we'd volunteered to work at the co-op, we would have reaped greater financial benefits. In the small town of Montpelier (population 8,035), the co-op was as big as any local supermarket.

Now we live in Portland, Oregon, and there are numerous similar food co-ops, mostly small and community based. These types of community-based nonprofits and health-food co-ops are the models familiar to Americans. While they have a good reputation, they are generally seen as inconsequential, economically speaking. To use the vernacular of the tech world, such co-ops are not "scalable" and therefore will remain small in size and scope.

But Mondragon, and other large co-ops around the world like Asiapro in the Philippines, exemplify another business model. Every bit as aggressive, every bit as competitive, and every bit as successful as large for-profit corporations, the Mondragon Cooperative offers a serious alternative to predatory capitalism that puts workers first, caters to the needs of customers, and, perhaps more importantly, establishes a business model that is fair, humane, and equitable.

Early economic models—from monarchy to hierarchy to capitalism—represent ways for the predatory and the acquisitive to rise to the top of the pile and get as much as they can. As such they foster the human traits of greed and aggression.

One way to consider the fundamental issue is to ask: *is the economy here to serve workers, or are workers here to serve those who own the economy?* The answer of old-fashioned capitalism— reaching all the way back to Gilgamesh's time in 2700 B.C.—is that workers are here to serve the economy and its owners.

But that can be changed—and it is being changed all over the world. It is entirely possible in twenty-first-century America for us to use the tools of technology and finance to spawn large numbers of Mondragon-like cooperatives right here.

If a $24 billion cooperative venture can be successfully established in the remote Basque region of northern Spain, surely it can be done in modern-day metropolises of the wealthiest nation on earth.

Conclusion:
Tag, You're It!

As nightfall does not come at once, neither does oppression.
In both instances, there's a twilight where everything
remains seemingly unchanged, and it is in such twilight
that we must be aware of change in the air, however
slight, lest we become unwitting victims of the darkness.

—William O. Douglas

Is PAST TRULY PROLOGUE?

In his introduction to an 1899 English-language edition of
Alexis de Tocqueville's 1835 classic *Democracy in America,* former
Alabama state senator John T. Morgan describes the formative
period of the "experimental" American republic:[1]

> Those liberties had been wrung from reluctant monarchs in
> many contests, in many countries, and were grouped into creeds
> and established in ordinances sealed with blood, in many great
> struggles of the people. They were not new to the people. They
> were consecrated theories, but no government had been pre-
> viously established for the great purpose of their preservation
> and enforcement. That which was experimental in our plan of
> government was the question whether democratic rule could be
> so organized and conducted that it would not degenerate into
> license and result in the tyranny of absolutism...

There was considerable concern during the Robber Baron
Era when Morgan wrote that the Rockefellers and Goulds and
Hearsts among us would ultimately end up an overwhelming rul-
ing class.

It was just two years after William Randolph Hearst had cabled his artist correspondent to Cuba, Frederick Remington, "You provide the pictures, and I'll provide the war."

Hearst came through on his end of the deal, and the Spanish-American War—started largely by his newspapers and the public sentiment they controlled—led many Americans to wonder if our nation would ever become the egalitarian democracy its Founders envisioned. A new aristocracy was rising up and, some said, had totally taken over not only our business and our press but our government as well.

De Tocqueville himself warned of it in his own introduction to his 1835 book that Morgan later wrote a second introduction for: "Men are not corrupted by the exercise of power or debased by the habit of obedience," he wrote, "but by the exercise of power which they believe to be illegal, and by obedience to a rule which they consider to be usurped and oppressive."[2]

Yet within a decade of Morgan's worrying concern that America was about to "degenerate" into the "tyranny of absolutism," Republican president Theodore Roosevelt rose up against the corporate monarchs who thought they ruled this country and went after them with an iron hammer. He smashed Rockefeller's Standard Oil Trust into more than 30 pieces. He called for minimum-wage and maximum-hour laws, famously calling for a "Square Deal" for every working American. He declared that every working person has the right to a "living wage," which he defined as enough to raise children, provide good housing, cover the costs of health care and retirement, and even ensure an annual vacation.

It would still be a few generations before Teddy Roosevelt's vision was accomplished during the presidency of another Republican, Dwight Eisenhower, but for more than half of all American workers that middle-class dream became real during the 30-year postwar era, coming to an end only when Ronald Reagan began his presidency by declaring war on organized labor by busting the PATCO air-traffic controllers union.

We've seen a lot of cycles in the history of this nation, a series of swings back and forth on the pendulum of oligarchy and democracy in our 230-plus years. In some ways today seems particularly bleak, when an individual hedge fund manger—a job that produces nothing of value for anybody—can suck out of our economy and take home in a single year more than $4 billion ($4,000,000,000.00) by betting that an investment vehicle held by pension funds and retirement trusts will fail. A small group of such individuals, in early 2010, paid themselves more than $140 billion—more than the sovereign debt of Greece, which ended up crushing that nation.

Yet if there are lessons in history, the first among them is that this too shall pass. Early advocates of abolition and suffrage never lived to see the fruits of their work, but an African-American president and a woman who nearly won the presidency would surely have both stunned and fulfilled them.

So the question today is: *Will our republic survive as a democracy?* Or will it continue to deteriorate into a corporate oligarchy, where all the forms and trappings are still in place but they're merely a decorative shell over a rotten, bloated, tiny group of billionaires who pull all the strings, own all the media (and every other industry of substance), and work all politics exclusively to their own benefit?

In an era when even the populist uprisings—the Tea Party demonstrations—are actually spawned from a Republican PR company's business plan and funded by oil billionaires, it's easy to be concerned.

The Biggest Lesson of History

As challenging as the task may seem, we're facing nothing compared with what the Founders took on; and Franklin Roosevelt famously told us that while great wealth may hate him, "I welcome their hatred." Presidents can lead on behalf of the people, but only when the people demand that they do so.

That's the biggest lesson of history. It took the excesses of the Tea Act of 1773—cutting to virtually nothing the taxes the East India Company paid on tea so that it could destroy its small colonial competitors—to provoke the colonists to commit the act of anti-corporate vandalism known as the Boston Tea Party. It took the excesses of the robber barons to provoke Teddy Roosevelt to challenge them. It took the nationwide economic destruction of the Republican Great Depression to motivate the people enough to support and encourage Franklin D. Roosevelt to institute—over three (and a fraction) presidential terms—the New Deal.

Our economy is in tatters, the result of more than 30 years of Reaganomics and Clintonomics. Our democracy is hanging by a thread, the result of 40 years of radical Supreme Court decisions steadily advancing the powers of corporations and suppressing the rights of individuals and their government. And our environment is trembling under the combined assault of the Industrial Revolution and nearly 7 billion bundles of human flesh.

It's the perfect time. We are clearly at a nexus, a threshold, a tipping point. If the past is any indicator, things will get worse before they get better, but in that tragedy will be both the catalyst and the seeds for a very positive future.

Now is the most important time for us all to be paying attention, to show up, and to wake up our friends, family, and neighbors. Because this nation is on the edge of a radical restart, a reboot.

Tag, you're it.

Acknowledgments

Safir Ahmed took on the unenviable job of editing this book on the fly as I was writing it during various trips and weekends and moments I could grab over the past year after I got off the air every day. It came to him in bits and pieces, sometimes inchoate, and he did a marvelous job of stitching together my many off-the-cuff writings. I'm deeply grateful for his work as the primary editor on this book.

Without the advocacy, insight, and tough editorial work of Johanna Vondeling at Berrett-Koehler and the brainstorming brilliance of my wife, Louise Hartmann, this book would not exist.

I'm particularly grateful to others at Berrett-Koehler who brought this book into being and made it work, both editorially, graphically, and in the marketplace. They include Richard Wilson, Dianne Platner, Jeevan Sivasubramaniam, marketing associate Jeremy Sullivan, senior sales manager Michael Crowley, sales manager Marina Cook, and publicist Katie Sheehan. And many thanks and much gratitude to a couple of real pros—Gary Palmatier and Elizabeth von Radics of Ideas to Images—for the book's design and copyediting.

Notes

Introduction: Back to the Future

1. Benson J. Lossing, *Our Country* (1877), http://www.publicbookshelf
   .com/public_html/Our_Country_vol_2/georgewas_bfb.html.

2. This section taken from Rosemary E. Bachelor, *Washington's
   American Made Inaugural Clothes,* http://americanhistory.suite101
   .com/article.cfm/washingtons-american-made-inaugural-clothes.

CHAPTER **1**

Bring My Job Home!

1. Peter S. Goodman, "The New Poor: Despite Signs of Recovery,
   Chronic Joblessness Rises," *New York Times,* February 21, 2010,
   http://www.nytimes.com/2010/02/21/business/economy/21unem
   ployed.html.

2. Keith Bradsher, "Defying Global Slump, China Has Labor Shortage," *New York Times,* February 26, 2010, http://www.nytimes.com/
   2010/02/27/business/global/27yuan.html.

3. Alexander Hamilton, *Report on the Subject of Manufactures: Made
   in His Capacity of Secretary of the Treasury,* December 5, 1791, http://
   www.archive.org/details/alexanderhamiltoocaregoog.

4. Peter Baker and Rachel Donadio, "Obama Wins More Food Aid but
   Presses African Nations on Corruption," *New York Times,* July 10,
   2009, http://www.nytimes.com/2009/07/11/world/europe/11prexy
   .html.

5. Editorial, "Tangled Trade Talks," *New York Times,* July 11, 2009,
   http://www.nytimes.com/2009/07/11/opinion/11sat1.html.

6. Ha-Joon Chang, *Bad Samaritans: The Myth of Free Trade and the Secret History of Capitalism* (New York: Bloomsbury Press, 2007). The ensuing discussion of Korea draws from this source.

7. See note 3 above. The ensuing discussion and quotations of Hamilton draw from this source.

CHAPTER **2**

Roll Back the Reagan Tax Cuts

1. This story was first noted in Thom Hartmann, *Threshold: The Crisis of Western Culture* (New York: Viking, 2009).

2. "University of Leicester Produces the First Ever World Map of Happiness," news release, July 29, 2006, http://www2.le.ac.uk/ ebulletin/news/press-releases/2000-2009/2006/07/nparticle .2006-07-28.2448323827.

3. Larry Beinhart, "Tax Cuts: Theology, Facts & Totally F**ked," Huffington Post, November 17, 2008, http://www.huffingtonpost .com/larry-beinhart/tax-cuts-theology-facts-t_b_144281.html.

4. Pittsburgh Post-Gazette, "Scaife Demands Documents from Post-Gazette," September 23, 2007, http://www.post-gazette.com/ pg/07266/819835-85.stm#ixzz0kTL6k84B.

5. Cenk Uygur, "Conservative Media vs. Progressive Media," Daily Kos, July 1, 2009, http://www.dailykos.com/story/2009/7/1/748854/ -Conservative-Media-vs.-Progressive-Media.

6. "The Heritage Foundation's 35th Anniversary: A History of Achievements," http://www.heritage.org/About/Our-History/ 35th-Anniversary.

7. "New 'Mandate for Leadership' Will Help Citizens Keep Politicians Honest," news release, January 10, 2005, http://www.heritage.org/ Research/Reports/2005/01/New-MANDATE-FOR-LEADERSHIP -Will-Help-Citizens-Keep-Politicians-Honest.

8. "The Impact of Higher Taxes: More Spending, Economic Stagnation, Fewer Jobs, and Higher Deficits," February 10, 1993, http://www .heritage.org/Research/Reports/1993/02/The-Impact-of-Higher

-Taxes-More-Spending-Economic-Stagnation-Fewer-Jobs-and -Higher-Deficits.

9. Bruce Bartlett, "The Futility of Raising Tax Rates," Cato Policy Analysis No. 192, http://www.cato.org/pubs/pas/pa-192.html.

10. Chandler, MacDonald, Stout, Schneiderman and Poe, Inc., dba The Newsletter Factory, http://www.nlf-pmr.com/html/about_us.html.

11. International Wholesale Travel, dba Sprayberry Travel, http://www .sprayberrytravel.com/about_company.htm.

12. The New England Salem Children's Village, www.salemchildrens village.org.

13. Barry C. Lynn, "Abolish Stock Options," *Harpers,* November 2008, http://harpers.org/media/pages/2008/11/pdf/HarpersMagazine -2008-11-0082251.pdf (requires subscription).

14. Peter Drier, "Meet UnitedHealth CEO Stephen Hemsley: Rich, Powerful, Not Yet Famous," Huffington Post, October 6, 2009, http://www.huffingtonpost.com/peter-dreier/meet-unitedhealth -ceo-ste_b_310674.html.

15. William A. Niskanen, "Chairman's Message: 'Starve the Beast' Does Not Work," CATO Policy Report March/April 2004, http://www .cato.org/pubs/policy_report/v26n2/cpr-26n2-2.pdf; and Jonathan Rauch, "Stoking the Beast: Cutting Taxes to Shrink Government Doesn't Work—and That Spells Trouble for the Conservative Movement," *Atlantic,* June 2006, http://www.theatlantic.com/ magazine/archive/2006/06/stoking-the-beast/4862.

CHAPTER **3**

Stop Them from Eating My Town

1. Thom Hartmann, *Unequal Protection: How Corporations Became "People"—and How You Can Fight Back,* 2nd ed. (San Francisco: Berrett-Koehler, 2010).

2. Mohan Guruswamy, Kamal Sharma, Jeevan Prakash Mohanty, and Thomas J. Korah, "FDI in India's Retail Sector: More Bad than

Good?" Center for Policy Alternatives, http://indiafdiwatch.org/fileadmin/India_site/10-FDI-Retail-more-bad.pdf.

3. http://en.wikipedia.org/wiki/Monopoly_(game).

4. Christopher Helman, "What the Top U.S. Companies Pay in Taxes: How Can It Be That You Pay More to the IRS Than General Electric?" *Forbes,* April 1, 2010, http://www.forbes.com/2010/04/01/ge-exxon-walmart-business-washington-corporate-taxes.html.

5. Hawken and I had this conversation when he was working on his article "Natural Capitalism" for *Mother Jones* magazine (published in the March/April 1997 issue). The article was later expanded to a book of the same name; see http://www.natcap.org.

6. David Barboza, "Chicago, Offering Big Incentives, Will Be Boeing's New Home," *New York Times,* May 11, 2001, http://www.nytimes.com/2001/05/11/business/chicago-offering-big-incentives-will-be-boeing-s-new-home.html?pagewanted=1.

7. Bob McIntyre, "Bush Policies Drive Surge in Corporate Tax Freeloading: 82 Big U.S. Corporations Paid No Tax in One or More Bush Years," Citizens for Tax Justice, September 22, 2004, http://www.ctj.org/corpfed04pr.pdf.

8. Stephen Moore and Dean Stansel, "How Corporate Welfare Won: Clinton and Congress Retreat from Cutting Business Subsidies," Cato Policy Analysis No. 254, May 15, 1996, http://www.cato.org/pubs/pas/pa-254.html.

9. David C. Korten, *The Post-corporate World* (San Francisco: Berrett-Koehler, 1999).

10. Borden Chemicals, noted by Noreena Hertz, PhD, in *The Silent Takeover* (London: Heinemann, 2001).

11. *New York Times,* September 21, 1995.

12. Donald L. Barlett and James B. Steele, "Corporate Welfare," *Time,* November 9, 1998, http://www.time.com/time/magazine/article/0,9171,989508,00.html.

13. Ibid.

14. Ibid.

15. Ibid.

16. Charles V. Bagli, "Companies Get Second Helping of Tax Breaks," *New York Times,* October 17, 1997, http://www.nytimes.com/1997/10/17/nyregion/companies-get-second-helping-of-tax-breaks .html?pagewanted=1.

17. Greg LeRoy, "No More Candy Store: States and Cities Making Job Subsidies Accountable" (Washington, DC: Good Jobs First, 1994), http://www.goodjobsfi rst.org/pdf/nmcs.pdf.

18. Ibid.

19. Joseph G. Lehman, "MEGA Program Shifts Jobs to Where They Are Needed Least," Mackinac Center for Public Policy, April 7, 1999, http://www.mackinac.org/1669.

20. See note 16 above.

21. "Overview & History, U.S. Small Business Administration," http://www.sba.gov/aboutsba/history/index.html.

CHAPTER **4**

An Informed and Educated Electorate

1. "Ted Koppel Assesses the Media Landscape," BBC World News, April 12, 2010, http://news.bbc.co.uk/2/hi/programmes/world _news_america/8616838.stm.

2. "Studio," Museum of Broadcast Communications, http://www .museum.tv/eotvsection.php?entrycode=studio.

3. Yochai Benler, "Ending the Internet's Trench Warfare," *New York Times,* March 20, 2010, http://www.nytimes.com/2010/03/21/opinion/21Benkler.html.

4. Wallace Turner, "Gov. Reagan Proposes Cutback in U. of California Appropriation; Would Impose Tuition Charge on Students from State; Kerr Weighs New Post," *New York Times,* January 7, 1967, cited in Gary K. Clabaugh, "The Educational Legacy of Ronald Reagan,"

NewFoundations.com, January 24, 2009, http://www.newfounda
tions.com/Clabaugh/CuttingEdge/Reagan.html#_edn3.

5. Steven V. Roberts, "Ronald Reagan Is Giving 'Em Heck, *New York Times,* October 25, 1970, cited in Clabaugh, "Educational Legacy."

6. Richard C. Paddock, "Less to Bank on at State Universities," *Los Angeles Times,* October 7, 2007, http://articles.latimes.com/2007/oct/07/local/me-newcompact7.

7. Gary K. Clabaugh, "The Educational Legacy of Ronald Reagan," NewFoundations.com, January 24, 2009, http://www.newfounda
tions.com/Clabaugh/CuttingEdge/Reagan.html#_edn3.

8. James C. Carter, *The University of Virginia: Jefferson Its Father, and His Political Philosophy: An Address Delivered upon the Occasion of the Dedication of the New Buildings of the University, June 14, 1898* (Ann Arbor: University of Michigan Library, 1898).

9. Albert Ellery Berch, ed., *The Writings of Thomas Jefferson,* vol. 2 (Washington, DC: Thomas Jefferson Memorial Association, 1905), http://www.constitution.org/tj/jeff02.txt.

CHAPTER **5**

Medicare "Part E"—for Everybody

1. "Wages and Benefits: A Long-term View," Kaiser Family Foundation, November 2009, http://www.kff.org/insurance/snapshot/chcmo
128080th.cfm.

2. "Premiums Soaring in Consolidated Health Insurance Market: Lack of Competition Hurts Rural States, Small Businesses," Health Care for America Now! May 2009, http://hcfan.3cdn.net/1b741c44183247
e6ac_20m6i6nzc.pdf.

3. Economist Intelligence Unit, "A New Ranking of the World's Most Innovative Countries," *Economist,* April 2009, http://graphics.eiu
.com/PDF/Cisco_Innovation_Complete.pdf.

4. T. R. Reid, *The Healing of America: A Global Quest for Better, Cheaper, and Fairer Health Care* (New York: Penguin Press, 2009).

5. Robert M. Ball, "Perspectives on Medicare," *Health Affairs* 14, no. 4 (1995), http://content.healthaffairs.org/cgi/reprint/14/4/62.pdf.

CHAPTER **6**

Make Members of Congress Wear NASCAR Patches

1. Kevin McCoy, "IRS Unlocks UBS Vault Hiding Americans Evading Taxes," *USA Today,* February 20, 2009, http://www.usatoday.com/money/industries/banking/2009-02-19-ubs-tax-evaders-irs_N.htm.

2. Jeffrey H. Birnbaum, "The Road to Riches Is Called K Street: Lobbying Firms Hire More, Pay More, Charge More to Influence Government," *Washington Post,* June 22, 2005, http://www.washingtonpost.com/wp-dyn/content/article/2005/06/21/AR2005062101632.html.

3. Ibid.

4. Anne C. Mulkern, "When Advocates Become Regulators: President Bush Has Installed More Than 100 Top Officials Who Were Once Lobbyists, Attorneys or Spokespeople for the Industries They Oversee," *Denver Post,* May 23, 2004, http://www.commondreams.org/headlines04/0523-02.htm.

5. Matt Apuzzo "Former Interior Official Gets Prison," *Washington Post,* June 26, 2007, http://www.washingtonpost.com/wp-dyn/content/article/2007/06/26/AR2007062600179.html.

6. See note 4 above.

7. Lyman J. Nash, ed. *Wisconsin Statutes 1919, Volume II: Embracing All General Statutes in Force at the Close of the General and Special Sessions of 1919, Consolidated and in Part Revised Pursuant to Sections 43.07, 43.03, 35.18 and 35.19 of These Statutes* (Madison: State of Wisconsin, 1919), sec. 4479a, 1771–1775, http://books.google.com/books?id=6ZCxAAAAMAAJ&pg=PA2299&lpg=PA2299&ots=WxkbUWGxMn&dq=wisconsin+1905+section+4479a&output=text.

8. "Ex-ministers in 'Cash for Influence' Row under Fire," BBC News, March 21, 2010, http://news.bbc.co.uk/2/hi/8578597.stm.

9. Patrick Wintour and Allegra Stratton, "Stephen Byers and Other Ex-ministers Suspended from Labour Party over Lobbying Allegations," March 23, 2010, http://www.guardian.co.uk/politics/2010/mar/23/stephen-byers-geoff-hoon-patricia-hewitt.

10. See note 8 above.

11. "Ca$hing In: More Than 900 Ex–Government Officials, Including 70 Former Members Of Congress, Have Lobbied for the Financial Services Sector in 2009," Public Citizen, http://www.citizen.org/congress/govt_reform/revolving/articles.cfm?ID=19092.

12. John Maynard Keynes, *The General Theory of Employment, Interest, and Money* (Amherst, NY: Prometheus Books, 1936, 1997).

13. Daniel Mica, "Consumers Are Moving Their Money to Credit Unions, Rising Membership Shows," January 6, 2010, Huffington Post, http://www.huffingtonpost.com/daniel-mica/consumers-are-moving----t_b_414190.html.

14. E-mail message received by the author from a listener. Reprinted verbatim with his permission.

CHAPTER **7**

Cool Our Fever

1. Jim Hansen, "State of the Wild: Perspective of a Climatologist," April 10, 2007, http://www.davidkabraham.com/Gaia/Hansen%20State%20of%20the%20Wild.pdf; also in Eva Fearn, ed., *State of the Wild 2008–2009: A Global Portrait of Wildlife, Wildlands, and Oceans* (Washington, DC: Island Press, 2008), p. 27.

2. Jad Mouawad and Andrew C. Revkin, "Saudis Seek Payments for Any Drop in Oil Revenues," *New York Times,* October 13, 2009, http://www.nytimes.com/2009/10/14/business/energy-environment/14oil.html.

3. Wallace S. Broecker, "CO_2 Arithmetic," *Science* 315 (2007): 1371; and comments in *Science* 316 (2007): 829; and Oliver Morton, "Is This What It Takes to Save the World?" *Nature* 447 (2007): 132.

4. Millennium Ecosystem Assessment, *Living Beyond Our Means: Natural Assets and Human Well-being, Statement from the Board,* March 2005, 5; and Jonathan A. Foley et al., "Global Consequences of Land Use," *Science* 309 (2005): 570.

5. James Lovelock, *Gaia: A New Look at Life on Earth,* 3rd ed. (New York: Oxford University Press, 2000).

6. http://en.wikipedia.org/wiki/Standby_power.

7. http://en.wikipedia.org/wiki/Electric_power_transmission.

8. "The 100.000 Roofs Programme," Renewable Energy Action, http://www.senternovem.nl/mmfiles/The%20100.000%20Roofs%20Programme_tcm24-117023.pdf.

9. Preben Maegaard, "Sensational German Renewable Energy Law and Its Innovative Tariff Principles," Folkecenter for Renewable Energy, http://www.folkecenter.dk/en/articles/EUROSUN2000-speech-PM.htm.

10. http://en.wikipedia.org/wiki/Solar_power_in_Germany.

11. "U.S. Nuclear Energy Plants," Nuclear Energy Institute, http://www.nei.org/resourcesandstats/nuclear_statistics/usnuclearpowerplants.

12. See note 10 above.

13. http://en.wikipedia.org/wiki/German_Renewable_Energy_Sources_Act.

14. Mark Landler, "Germany Debates Subsidies for Solar Industry," *New York Times,* May 16, 2008, http://www.nytimes.com/2008/05/16/business/worldbusiness/16solar.html.

15. Jim Tankersley and Don Lee, "China Takes Lead in Clean-power Investment: U.S. Falls to No. 2 in Funding for Such Alternative Sources as Wind and Solar," *Los Angeles Times,* March 25, 2010, http://www.latimes.com/business/la-fi-energy-china25-2010mar25,0,356464.story.

CHAPTER **8**

They Will Steal It!

1. Greg Mortenson, *Three Cups of Tea: One Man's Mission to Promote Peace One School at a Time* (New York: Penguin Books, 2007); and its sequel, *Stones into Schools: Promoting Peace with Books, Not Bombs, in Afghanistan and Pakistan* (New York: Viking Adult, 2009).

2. Thomas Jefferson to C. W. F. Dumas, February 12, 1788, http://books.google.com/books?id=2D0gAAAAIAAJ&pg=PA187&lpg=PA187&dq=%22Virginia,+I+think,+will+be+of+this+number%22+jefferson&source=bl&ots=g0B3NRKzou&sig=zjzsc-qRDYzEG4xVBjNDhMuC8FY&hl=en&ei=1jLZS8nrC4n-tQPIk_yoAQ&sa=X&oi=book_result&ct=result&resnum=3&ved=0CBEQ6AEwAg#v=onepage&q&f=false.

3. Alexander Hamilton, Federalist Papers (No. 29), http://www.foundingfathers.info/federalistpapers/fed29.htm.

4. Thomas Jefferson to James Monroe, June 18, 1813, http://books.google.com/books?id=a080G7xRRBUC&pg=PR62&lpg=PR62&dq=Thomas+Jefferson+to+James+Monroe,+June+18,+1813&source=bl&ots=npJJykbZFd&sig=cImEO4ScklK0BpOn3VvxjIMyrA4&hl=en&ei=jJ_5S4HyNYXeNd2v9YMI&sa=X&oi=book_result&ct=result&resnum=1&ved=0CBcQ6AEwAA#v=onepage&q=Thomas%20Jefferson%20to%20James%20Monroe%2C%20June%2018%2C%201813&f=false.

5. Dwight D. Eisenhower, Farewell Address to the Nation, January 17, 1961, http://mcadams.posc.mu.edu/ike.htm.

6. Benjamin H. Friedman, "The US Should Cut Military Spending in Half," *Christian Science Monitor*, April 27, 2009, http://www.cato.org/pub_display.php?pub_id=10152.

7. Stephen Budiansky, "Truth Extraction: A Classic Text on Interrogating Enemy Captives Offers a Counterintuitive Lesson on the Best Way to Get Information, *Atlantic*, June 2005, http://www.theatlantic.com/magazine/archive/2005/06/truth-extraction/3973.

CHAPTER **9**

Put Lou Dobbs out to Pasture

1. Jack Welch, "Outsourcing Is Forever," http://www.welchway.com/ Management/US-Economy-and-Government-Policy/Economic -Trends-and-Phenonmenon/Outsourcing-is-Forever.aspx.

2. September 28, 2007, http://www.youtube.com/watch?v=oqx88 MyUSck.

3. Liz Hull and Lee Sorrell, "The Image Microsoft Doesn't Want You to See: Too Tired to Stay Awake, the Chinese Workers Earning Just 34p an Hour," *Daily Mail,* April 18, 2010, http://www.dailymail.co.uk/ news/article-1266643/Microsofts-Chinese-workforce-tired-stay -awake.html

4. *Meet the Press,* September 14, 2003, http://www.msnbc.msn.com/ id/3080244.

5. "The Employment Situation—April 2010," news release, Bureau of Labor Statistics, May 7, 2010, http://www.bls.gov/news.release/pdf/ empsit.pdf.

6. "Hispanics and Arizona's New Immigration Law," Pew Research Center Publications, April 29, 2010, http://pewresearch.org/ pubs/1579/arizona-immigration-law-fact-sheet-hispanic-popula tion-opinion-discrimination.

CHAPTER **10**

Wal-Mart Is *Not* a Person

1. Robert Barnes, "Justices to Review Campaign Finance Law Constraints," *Washington Post,* June 30, 2009, http://www.washington post.com/wp-dyn/content/article/2009/06/29/AR2009062903997 .html.

2. *Citizens United v. Federal Election Commission,* 558 U.S. __ (2010), http://www.supremecourt.gov/opinions/09pdf/08-205.pdf.

3. David D. Kirkpatrick, "In a Message to Democrats, Wall St. Sends Cash to G.O.P.," *New York Times,* February 7, 2010, http://www .nytimes.com/2010/02/08/us/politics/08lobby.html.

4. Bill Moyers and Michael Winship, "What Are We Bid for American Justice?" Huffington Post, February 19, 2010, http://www.huffington post.com/bill-moyers/what-are-webid-for-ameri_b_469335.html.

Conclusion: Tag, You're It!

1. John T. Morgan, introduction to *Democracy in America,* rev ed., by Alexis de Tocqueville (New York: Colonial Press, 1835, 1899), http:// books.google.com/books?printsec=frontcover&id=_OgJAAAAIA AJ#v=onepage&q&f=false.

2. Alexis de Tocqueville, *The Republic of the United States of America, and Its Political Institutions, Reviewed and Examined* (New York: A. S. Barnes, 1862).

Index

Abramoff, Jack, 100, 103

Afghanistan, 62, 66, 141–142, 150

airwaves ownership, 66–67

Alexander Hamilton's 11-point plan
background, 2–3, 10
implementations, 21, 24–25, 27
text of, 3–9

Alito, Samuel, 172, 178, 180

alternative energy, 123–128, 132–135, 137

amending the Constitution, 111, 187–189

American Federation of Labor (AFL), 90

American Medical Association (AMA), 90–91

American Recovery and Reinvestment Act (2009), 16–20

American Revolution, 2, 175, 202

Amin, Idi, 139

Anschutz, Philip, 39, 41, 42, 48

Anthem Blue Cross, 184

anti-intellectualism, 12, 75–76, 79

antitrust legislation, 11, 44, 54–56

Aristotelian worldview, 131–132

Austin v. Michigan Chamber of Commerce, 172–173, 180

automobiles, flex-fuel, 127–128, 135, 137

Baker, Dean, 115

balance of power, 167–168

Ball, Robert M., 89–91

bankruptcy laws, 95

banks
community credit unions over, 119–122
industry lobbying, 101, 111
owning the Federal Reserve, 112–113
participating in solar energy programs, 124, 133, 134
raising savings interest rates, 30
reform efforts, 114, 184
savings-and-loan crisis, 37, 120
state-run, 114
stock market trading by, 115, 117–118
2008 financial crisis and, 30, 100, 183
using local, 51–52, 54, 118–119
wealthy using Swiss, 34, 43, 101

Bartlett, Bruce, 42

Beck, Glenn, 71, 147

Beinhart, Larry, 37

Bennett, William, 79

big-box retailers, 51–53

big business. *See* corporations

Bill of Rights, 144, 169, 176, 178, 189

Bipartisan Campaign Reform Act (McCain-Feingold), 110, 171, 172, 173, 180

Birnbaum, Jeffrey, 101–102

Boeing Company, 58

Boston Ports Act (British), 175

Boston Tea Party, 2, 175, 202

BP oil spill, 106, 131

Brazil, 127

British East India Company, 2, 175, 202

broadcast news, 41, 65–69

Bush, George H. W., 3, 18, 21, 27, 37, 46, 56, 157, 165

Bush, George W., 19, 95, 166, 172, 180
appointment of former lobbyists, 102–104
defense spending, 62, 147–149
embracing "free trade," 3, 10, 21, 27, 56
national debt under, 116–117, 147

Bush, George W. (continued)
    tax cuts by, 11, 35, 38, 46, 47, 48, 88,
        195
    2008 economic crisis legacy, 18, 19,
        113, 114
    war and torture, 149–150
business. See corporations; small/local
    businesses

cable industry, 73–74
Caesar, Julius, 125
California, 75–76, 77, 93, 100, 184
campaign finance reform
    Austin case furthering, 172–173
    Bipartisan Campaign Reform Act
        (McCain-Feingold), 110, 171, 172,
        173
    Citizens United case derailing, 12,
        30–31, 110–111, 170–171, 181–182,
        184
    historical model for, 107–108
Canada, 94
cap-and-trade-program, 137–138
capital gains, 38, 50
capitalism, 95, 193, 197
carbon tax/credits, 137–138
Carnegie, Andrew, 56, 83
cars, flex-fuel, 127–128, 135, 137
Carter, James C., 77–78
Carter, Jimmy, 31, 47, 61, 125
Cartesian worldview, 131–132
Cash for Clunkers programs, 18, 28
Cato Institute, 11, 41, 42, 46, 48, 58, 148
Centers for Medicare and Medicaid
    Services (CMS), 92, 104
CEOs, 43–46, 49–50, 87, 166, 193
chain stores, 51–53
Chang, Ha-Joon, 22, 23
chartermongering, 175–176
Chávez, César, 161
Cheney, Dick, 102, 107, 147, 148, 150, 159
China, 10, 20, 21, 28, 135–136, 158
citizenry. See electorate

Citizens United v. Federal Election
    Commission
    background of, 170–172
    concurring opinions, 182–183
    corporate "free-speech" and, 14, 30,
        170, 172–174, 177, 178–183
    damage done following, 183–186
    derailing campaign finance re-
        forms, 12, 30–31, 110–111, 170–171,
        181–182, 184
    foreign corporations and, 177, 186
    majority decision, 173–174, 176
    minority dissent, 177–182
    "natural persons" debate in, 174,
        178–179
    opinions online, 180
    significance of decision, 14, 30, 170,
        172, 180–182, 184–186
    superseding the decision, 186–189
citizenship, 162, 164
Civil War, 115, 117, 140, 174, 187
Clinton, Bill, 3, 95, 148, 202
    deregulation by, 56, 68, 73, 115
    embracing "free trade," 10, 21, 25, 27,
        157, 158
    taxes under, 11, 35, 37, 41–42, 46, 47,
        48
Clinton, Hillary, 170–171
clothing industry, colonial, 1–2
Cobb, David, 188
Commodity Futures Modernization Act
    (CFMA), 100
commons, 66, 68, 73–74
community credit unions, 30, 64,
    119–122
conservatives
    Internet scrubbing by, 76
    spin on tax cuts, 34, 38–42, 48
    talk radio, 68, 71–72
    worldview of, 171
consumer spending, 159, 165–166
cooperatives, 14, 119–120, 192–194,
    196–198
Cornyn, John, 183–184
corporate oligarchy
    Citizens United furthering, 14, 30–31,
        170

and the conservative worldview,
171–172
constitutional amendment to halt,
111, 188, 189
historical perspective of, 175–178,
199–201
as threat to democracy, 201
corporate personhood
and campaign finance reform, 12,
30–31, 110–111, 170–171, 181–182,
184
Citizens United and "free-speech
rights," 14, 30, 170, 172–174, 177,
178–183
constitutional amendment to prohibit, 31, 187–189
"natural persons" debate, 174,
178–179, 189
and *Santa Clara,* 14, 169–170, 176,
189
*See also Citizens United v. Federal
Election Commission*
corporations
benefiting from defense spending,
147–148
booming under Reagan, 11, 44
call to transform American, 195–198
capitalizing on tax loopholes, 61–62,
63
CEOs, 43–46, 49–50, 87, 166, 193
controlling health care, 82–83, 86,
87–88
devastating local economies, 51–53
existing for shareholder wealth, 45,
49–50, 195–196
Founding Fathers wary of, 175–178
mission of, 43–44, 45, 196
outsourcing mania, 155–160
paying for pollution, 129–130
shareholders as first priority, 30,
43–46, 159, 179, 195
tax avoidance by, 57–62
worker-owned, 14, 192–194, 196–198
See also corporate oligarchy; corporate personhood; lobbyists;
monopolies
credit trap, 166–167
credit unions, 30, 64, 119–122
currency, 8, 112–113, 119, 125

Darling, Alistair, 109
Davis, Gray, 100
defense spending, 143, 147–148, 150
Delaware, 176
DeLay, Tom, 99–100, 101
"democracy," 140–142, 181, 199–201
Democracy in America (de Tocqueville),
140, 199
Democrats, 18, 31, 47, 87–88, 162–163,
183–184
Denmark, 33–34, 128, 135, 138
deregulation, 68, 73–74, 115–118, 120
developed countries. *See* industrialized
nations
dividends, 38, 45, 46, 50, 196
draft, 143, 145, 146, 151
Dred Scott v. Sanford, 187
duty. *See* tariffs

East India Company, 2, 175, 202
economic crisis (2008), 17–20, 28, 100,
113, 114
economic health
balance of power, 167, 168
chain stores destroying, 51–53
credit undermining, 166–167
Hamilton's plan for, 24–27
manufacturing as key to, 10, 26
myth of "service economy," 10, 26,
157
New Deal, 18–21, 202
"supply-side" insanity, 164–166
tax cuts damaging, 34–38, 40, 42,
46–49
through cooperatives, 14, 119–120,
192–194, 196–198
vision to restore, 28–31
See also "free trade"; jobs; protectionism; subsidies; tariffs
economic models, 193, 197
economic stimulus bill, 17–20
education
purpose of, 78–79
Reagan's California cutbacks, 12,
75–76

education *(continued)*
  spreading democracy through,
    141–142
  vision of free, 11–12, 74–75, 77–80,
    145
Eisenhower, Dwight D., 31, 36, 49, 62,
    141, 146, 148, 200
electorate
  access to education, 74–79
  as "consumers," 159, 165–166
  encouraging savings by, 30
  lack of credible news for, 68–69
  preferring infotainment over news,
    65–66
  providing social safety net for,
    81–84, 87, 94–96
  right to choice in media content,
    73–74
  supporting an informed/educated,
    79–80
electricity, 126, 127, 128, 132–135
11-point plan. *See* Alexander Hamilton's
    11-point plan
Employee Free Choice Act, 167
employee-owned cooperatives, 14,
    192–194, 196–198
England, 2, 10, 21, 108–109, 117, 167, 175
Enron, 100
entrepreneurialism, 62–64, 77, 81–82,
    96, 97–99. *See also* small/local
    businesses
environmental impact
  alternative energy, 123–128, 132–135,
    137
  carbon tax/credits, 137–138
  earth as an organism, 131–132
  Millennium Ecosystem Assessment,
    130–131
  pollution, 126, 129–133, 186
  tariffs to offset industry, 29, 137
EPA (U.S. Environmental Protection
    Agency), 104, 186
Equal Time Rule, 67
Europe, 34, 49, 83, 127, 138, 191–192
externalizing costs, 129–131

Fairness Doctrine, 66–68
FDA (U.S. Food and Drug
    Administration), 103–104
Federal Election Commission (FEC),
    171, 172. *See also Citizens United v.
    Federal Election Commission*
federal highway funds, 61
Federal Reserve, 112–114
financial services industry, 111–112. *See
    also* banks
First Amendment. *See* free-speech
    rights
"flat world," 159
flex-fuel cars, 127–128, 135, 137
foreign corporations, free speech and,
    177, 186
foreign policy, 13, 140–143, 150–151
Founding Fathers, 24–28, 143–145,
    175–178, 189, 200. *See also*
    Alexander Hamilton's 11-point plan
Fourteenth Amendment, 174, 187–189
Fox "News," 41, 68
France, 73–74
free-speech rights
  Citizens United and corporate, 14,
    30, 170, 172–174, 177–183
  extended to foreign corporations,
    177, 186
  power of lobbyists and, 109–111, 174
"free trade"
  Asian nations successfully rejecting,
    22, 24
  high cost of, 20–21
  misguided embrace of, 10, 21, 25,
    157–159
  protectionism and tariffs over, 24–28
  working class dismantled by, 10, 157
Friedman, Benjamin, 148
Friedman, Milton, 44, 55, 56
Friedman, Thomas L., 22, 24, 31, 158–159

Gandhi, Mahatma, 2
gasoline tax, 129
General Agreement on Tariffs and
    Trade (GATT), 25, 157

Germany, 123–124, 133–135, 140–141, 147, 150, 164

Ghanta, Praveen, 84

Giuliani, Rudy, 60

"globalization," 157, 158–159

government
  break with the Supreme Court, 187
  citizenship and public services, 162
  cuts in education, 76
  deregulation, 68, 73–74, 115–118, 120
  and the Federal Reserve, 112–114
  foreign policy, reengineering, 13, 140–143, 150–151
  fostering industry, 27
  lobbyists and, 99–104
  monetary system, 111–114, 117–118
  political system integrity, 185–186
  reconciliation/majority rule, 88
  regulatory agencies, 102–104, 107
  reining in corporate control of, 107–111
  role in economic crisis, 18–19
  social safety net, 81–84, 87, 94–96
  taxes and size of, 11, 41–42, 46–48
  See also campaign finance reform; military; subsidies

Government Accountability Office (GAO), 113–114

Gramm, Phil, 100–101, 117–118

Gramm-Lech-Bliley Act, 117

Great Depression, 18, 37, 38, 62, 116, 202

Great Tax Con, 38–43, 48–50

Greenspan, Alan, 35, 38, 156–157, 166

Gregory, Dick, 13, 139–140

Griles, J. Steven, 102–103

Gulf oil spill, 106, 131

Halliburton, 29, 62, 106, 147

Hamilton, Alexander, 2–10, 21, 24–28, 136, 144

Hartmann, Louise, 43, 76–77, 82, 98, 120, 123, 191, 193, 196

Hawaii, 94

Hawken, Paul, 57, 58

HCA, 104

health care
  extending Medicare to all, 12, 88–93
  part of social safety net, 81–82, 94–96
  reform of, 87–88, 93
  universal health care (UHC), 83–86, 89–91, 93–94
  U.S. lagging behind in, 83–87

Health Care for America Now report, 82–83

health insurance, 12, 82–83, 86–88, 91, 184

Hearst, William Randolph, 200–201

Hemsley, Stephen J., 45

Henry VII, King, 21

Heritage Foundation, 37, 39–41, 111

Hertz, Noreena, 59n

higher education
  Jefferson's vision of free, 11–12, 74–75, 77–80, 145
  Reagan's California cutbacks, 12, 75–76

Hinsdale, Daniel, 2

Holmstead, Jeffrey, 104

Hoover, Herbert, 49, 62, 116, 117, 136, 146

housing-market bubble, 37, 116, 157

Huffington, Arianna, 119

Hunger Mountain Cooperative, 196

illegal hiring, 13, 153–155, 162, 164

immigration reform, 13, 153–155, 159, 160–164

India, 2, 53–54, 155–156

industrialized nations
  alternative energy initiatives, 123–124
  competitive cable/phone service, 73–74
  free higher education, 77
  income-tax rates, 33–34
  oil-drilling safeguards, 107
  prohibitions on retail chains, 53–54
  protectionism, 21–24
  universal health care, 83–86, 90, 94
  worker-owner cooperative, 192–195, 198
  workers on board of directors, 14

industry sector, lobbyist investments by, 105–106

infrastructure building, 8–9, 148, 167

innovation, 7–8, 77, 81–84, 95–96

insurance, health, 12, 82–83, 86–88, 91, 184

insurance mandate system, 84, 86

interest rates, 30, 114, 119

Internet scrubbing, 76

investment, 116

"investor class," 166, 201

Iraq, 62, 66, 125, 141, 146, 149–150, 159, 175

Ireland, 77, 86

Japan, 24, 28, 140–141, 147

Jefferson, Thomas, 9, 11–12, 25, 26, 74–75, 77–79, 143–146, 178

jobs
    cracking down on illegal hiring, 13, 153–155, 161–164
    economic stimulus package and, 17–20
    fair wages, 160–163, 165, 167, 200
    Hamilton's plan for creating, 25–28
    history of labor reforms, 160–161
    lowering Social Security age to increase, 163–164
    outsourcing, 155–160
    protectionism to boost, 21–24, 27–28
    to reboot the economy, 28
    "service economy," 10, 26, 157
    "talent insourcing," 156
    unemployment statistics, 161
    worker-owned cooperatives, 14, 192–194, 196–198

Johnson, Lyndon B., 31, 36, 88, 89, 91

judicial elections, 185–186

Kennedy, Anthony, 172, 173–174, 178

Kennedy, John F., 31, 89, 141

Kenya, 22

Keynes, John Maynard, 18–19, 20, 26, 115

Knox, Henry, 1, 2

Koppel, Ted, 69

Korten, David C., 58

Kristol, William, 41

labor reform, 160–161, 200

labor unions
    barred from campaign contributions, 171
    decline in, 162, 196
    fighting illegal immigration, 161
    general benefits of, 167
    Reagan busting up, 164, 165, 196, 200
    to strengthen the middle class, 164–165, 167–168

Laffer, Art, 165

Lambert, Charles, 103

Lay, Ken, 100

Limbaugh, Rush, 68, 71

Lincoln, Abraham, 24, 187

lobbyists
    appointed to regulatory agencies, 102–104
    British lobbying sting, 108–109
    and corporate free speech "rights," 109–111, 174
    as corporate investment, 99
    link to Congress, 99–102, 111–112
    overview on spending by, 104–106
    reining in control of government by, 107–111
    statistics on growth/salaries, 101–102

local business. *See* small/local businesses

local economies, 51–54, 64

Lovelock, James, 131

Luntz, Frank, 42

Lynn, Barry C., 44, 95

Magie, Elizabeth, 56

majority rule, 88

Mandate for Leadership (Heritage Foundation), 40

manufacturing
    in colonial America, 1–2, 10
    damaged by free trade and deregulation, 25, 27–28, 55

freed from the burden of health care, 12
Hamilton's plan for, 25–27, 136
as source of real wealth, 10, 26
tariffs to support, 29, 138
Marshall, John, 178
Maslow, Abraham, 142
Massachusetts, 94
McCain, John, 171
McCain-Feingold Act (Bipartisan Campaign Reform Act), 110, 171, 172, 180
McGuire, William, 45
media
breaking up monopolies in, 70–74, 79–80
cable networks, opening use of, 73–74
committed to infotainment, 65–66
devolution of broadcast news, 66–69
owned by the wealthy, 38–39, 41, 159
spin on tax cuts, 34, 38–42, 48
Medicare, 12, 88–93
mergers and acquisitions, 44, 55, 63
Mexico, 29, 126, 157, 159, 161, 168
middle class
cost of higher education, 77
dismantled by free trade/deregulation, 10, 95
history of the, 26, 37, 160–161, 200
taxes and the, 17, 37, 42
tightening the labor market to stabilize, 163, 164
unions for a strong, 164–165, 168
See also working class
Milchen, Jeff, 188
military
atrocities committed by, 149–150
benefits of the draft, 143, 145, 146, 151
defense spending, 141, 143, 147–148, 150
Founders' debate over, 143–145
reining in the, 13, 140–143, 150–151
tied to oil dependency, 142–143
Millennium Ecosystem Assessment, 130–131
mission, 43–44, 45, 196

Mondragon Cooperative, 14, 192–195, 197
Mondragon University, 194–195
monetary system, 111–114, 117–118
monopolies
breaking up media, 70–74, 79–80
chartermongering, 175–176
historical perspective on, 11, 44, 55–56, 175–176, 200, 202
India's laws against, 53–54
"monopoly capitalism," 95
Monopoly game, 56
Moon, Sun Myung, 39, 42, 48
Morgan, John Pierpont, 56
Morgan, John T., 199, 200
Mortenson, Greg, 141–142
Move to Amend, 188–189
movie studio system, 70
Moyers, Bill, 185
Murdoch, Rupert, 39, 41, 42, 48

"natural persons," 174, 178–179, 189
network television, 65, 67, 68, 71, 159
New Deal, 18, 19, 20–21, 202
news industry, 38–39, 41, 65–69, 200
Niskanen, William A., 46, 47–48
Nixon, Richard M., 31, 36, 89, 125, 147
nonprofits, 193, 196
North American Free Trade Agreement (NAFTA), 25, 29, 157
North Dakota, 114
nuclear power, 124, 130, 133, 134

Obama, Barack, 22, 47, 56, 62
and corporate political power, 30–31, 114n, 183–184
health-care reform, 87–88, 92, 93
stimulus bill, 17–19
support of free trade, 21, 28
O'Connor, Sandra Day, 186
oil dependency
alternative energy to decrease, 132–136
BP oil spill, 106, 131

oil dependency *(continued)*
  implementing carbon tax, 137–138
  making polluters pay, 129–132
  military tied to, 142–143
  other nations sloughing, 123–124,
    133–136
  Reagan strengthening, 125n
  stripping oil of strategic value,
    124–127
  tariffs to decrease, 128, 137, 138
  transportation driving, 126–128
OPEC (Organization of Petroleum
  Exporting Countries), 126
"original sin," 171–172

Pakistan, 141–142, 143, 150
Paramount Pictures, 70
Park Chung-hee, 23
Patient Protection and Affordable Care
  Act, 87
pharmaceutical industry, 87–88, 93,
  103–104, 184
Pickens, T. Boone, 56, 127
Pittsburgh Tribune-Review (newspaper),
  38–39
plutocracy, corporate. *See* corporate
  oligarchy
political system integrity, 185–186. *See
  also Citizens United v. Federal
  Election Commission*
pollution, 126, 129–133, 186
post-Reagan era
  abandoning America's legacy of suc-
    cess, 3, 27–28
  misguided embrace of "free trade,"
    10, 21, 25, 157
  possible demise of democracy in,
    170, 202
  social class rigidity, 195
  taxes in the, 11, 35–36, 38, 49
  See also "free trade"
"predatory plutocracy," 170
Prime Time Access Rule, 71
profits, 43–44, 45, 66, 82–83, 129–130,
  196
progressives, 72, 159, 160–163, 168

proprietary trading, 118, 119
protectionism
  abandoning "free trade" to, 20, 21
  creating jobs, 28–30
  in Hamilton's plan, 24–27
  South Korea's success through, 21–24
public-service announcements (PSAs),
  67
public-service broadcasting mandates,
  66, 67
Pulitzer, Joseph, 170

radio, 66–68, 71–72
Rand, Ayn, 55, 56, 156
Ratner, Ellen, 65
Rauch, Jonathan, 48
raw materials, 4–5, 7, 25, 28
Reagan, Ronald, 3, 45, 63, 89, 166, 170,
  202
  deregulation under, 11, 44, 54–56, 73,
    95, 115, 120
  education cutbacks, 12, 75–76, 79
  Fairness Doctrine rolled back by,
    66–68
  "free trade" proponent, 21, 25, 27, 28,
    29, 157
  against Medicare, 90
  military spending by, 147
  strengthening oil dependency, 125n
  "supply-side economics," 165
  supporting illegal immigration, 13
  tax cuts by, 10–11, 35, 37, 40, 42, 43,
    46–50, 88, 137, 195–196
  as union buster, 164, 165, 196, 200
real estate bubble, 37, 116, 157
reconciliation, 88
Reconstruction Finance Corporation
  (RFC), 62
regulatory agencies, 102–104, 107
Reich, Robert B., 60
Renewable Energies Law (Germany),
  133–134
Report on the Subject of Manufactures
  (Hamilton), 3, 21, 24–27

Republican Party
 capitalizing on economic recovery
  act, 18
 and the *Citizens United* decision,
  183–184
 Great Depression of the, 18, 37, 38,
  62, 116, 202
 recent populist wedge in, 147, 159
 Republican Five, 172, 176
 tax cut damage by, 37, 38, 47
 See also conservatives
retail industry, 51–53
Revolutionary War, 2, 175, 202
Ricardo, David, 35
right wing. *See* conservatives
Rite of the First Night, 191–192, 194, 196
Robber Baron Era, 14, 107, 160, 169–170,
 199–200, 202
Roberts, John G., 170, 172, 173, 178, 180,
 182
Rockefeller, John D., 36, 56, 175, 199, 200
Roman Empire, 125
Romney, Mitt, 56
Roofs Program, 100.000 (Germany),
 133–135
Roosevelt, Franklin D., 18, 19, 20, 47, 117,
 136, 201–202
Roosevelt, Theodore, 11, 56, 171, 200, 202

Salem International, 98, 123, 196
Samsung, 22
Sanders, Bernie, 61, 101
*Santa Clara County v. Southern Pacific
 Railroad,* 14, 169–170, 176, 189
Saudi Arabia, 125–126, 128–129, 139
savings, 34–35
savings, personal, 30
savings-and-loan crisis, 37, 120
savings bonds, 30
SBA (Small Business Administration),
 62–63
Scaife, Richard Mellon, 38–39, 41, 42, 48
Scalia, Antonin, 111, 172, 178, 182
Schwarzenegger, Arnold, 76, 93, 100

Scully, Thomas A., 104
Second Amendment, 145
Securities Turnover Excise Tax (STET),
 115–117
"service economy," 10, 26, 157
shareholders, 30, 43–46, 159, 179, 195
Sherman Antitrust Act, 11, 44, 54–56,
 64, 95, 118
single-payer health care, 84
Small Business Administration (SBA),
 62–63
small/local businesses
 banks and community credit unions,
  118–122
 encouraging, 51–53, 62–64
 free from political influence activities, 99
 freed from the burden of health
  care, 12
 India's laws supporting, 53–54
 Reagan's demise of, 11, 54–55, 95
Smith, Adam, 10
social capital, 194
social rigidity, 195–196
social safety net, 81–84, 87, 94–96
Social Security, 89, 91, 163–164
solar power, 123–124, 132–135
South Korea, 21–24
Spanish-American War, 115, 117, 200
speculation, 115–118
state-funded higher education, 75–77
state health-care systems, 93–94
state-run banks, 114
states, corporate friendly, 58–60,
 175–176
STET (Securities Turnover Excise Tax),
 115–117
Stevens, John Paul, 177–182
stimulus bill, 17–20
stock market, 37, 114–118, 166
stock options, 42, 45–46, 49–50
stockholders, 30, 43–46, 159, 179, 195
Stockman, David, 165

studio system, 70

subsidies
    of big business, 57–62
    to break oil dependency, 128, 135
    in Hamilton's plan, 5–6, 24, 25
    Japan's auto industry, 24
    returning to, 20, 29

superstores, 51–53

"supply-side economics," 165–166

Taft-Hartley Act, 164, 167, 171

"talent insourcing," 156

Taliban, 141–142

talk radio, 68, 71–72

tariffs
    to decrease oil dependency, 128, 137,
        138
    environmental impact, 29
    in Hamilton's plan, 3–4, 7, 25, 27, 136
    returning to, 20, 27–29

tax cuts
    call to roll back, 48–50
    capital gains/dividends, 38, 46, 50,
        196
    favoring the wealthy, 36–38, 49,
        195–196
    Great Tax Con, 38–43, 48–50
    increasing the size of government,
        11, 46–48
    2009 middle-class, 17–18

taxes
    America's unequal system, 34–36
    benefits of, 36–38, 136–137
    carbon tax, 137–138
    closing loopholes, 61–62, 63
    Europe's pro-worker approach to,
        33–34
    gasoline tax, 129
    increasing the tax base, 163–164, 167
    raising upper class, 10, 42–43, 48–50
    and size of government, 11, 41–42,
        46–48
    STET (Securities Turnover Excise
        Tax), 115–117
    tax avoidance, 39, 41, 42, 57–62

top marginal tax rate, 36–37, 42, 49
    and "wage inflation," 35

Tea Act (British), 2, 175, 202

Tea Party, 30, 95, 157, 201

telecommunications, 73–74

Telecommunications Act of 1996, 68

television, 41, 65–69, 71, 159

Thomas, Clarence, 111, 172, 178

Tillman Act, 110, 171

Tocqueville, Alexis de, 140, 199, 200

top marginal tax rate, 36–37, 42, 49

Toyota, 24

trade
    in Asian countries, 20–25
    England's Tudor Plan, 10, 21
    Founding Fathers' wisdom on,
        24–28
    in Hamilton's plan, 3–8
    pulling out of trade agreements, 29
    See also "free trade"; tariffs

trade agreements, 25, 29

transportation, 8–9, 126–129, 137, 167

Troy, Daniel E., 103–104

True Cost blog, 84

Truman, Harry, 89, 90, 94, 164

trusts. *See* monopolies

Tudor Plan (England), 10, 21

Twenty-sixth Amendment, 187

2008 economic crisis, 17–20, 28, 100,
    113, 114

two-tier health care, 84, 86

UBS, 101

UFW (United Farm Workers), 161

Uganda, 139

unemployment, 161

Unequal Protection (Hartmann), 51, 57,
    101, 169

unions. *See* labor unions

United Farm Workers (UFW), 161

universal health care (UHC), 83–86,
    89–91, 93–94

University of California, 12, 75

University of Virginia, 11, 75, 77–78

upper class. *See* corporate oligarchy; wealthy

U.S. Chamber of Commerce, 105, 106, 174, 184

U.S. Congress, lobbyists and, 99–102, 111–112

U.S. Constitution
    Bill of Rights, 144, 169, 176, 178, 189
    corporate personhood and, 169–170, 187–189
    Fourteenth Amendment, 174, 187–189
    movement to amend the, 111, 187–189
    Second Amendment, 145
    Twenty-sixth Amendment, 187
    See also free-speech rights

U.S. Department of Agriculture (USDA), 103

U.S. Department of Education, 79

U.S. Environmental Protection Agency (EPA), 104, 186

U.S. Food and Drug Administration (FDA), 103–104

U.S. savings bonds, 30

U.S. Supreme Court
    amending a decision of, 186–189
    Austin limiting corporate political activities, 172–173, 180
    Dred Scott decision superseded by Lincoln, 187
    legacy of *Santa Clara*, 14, 169–170, 176, 189
    Republican Five, 172, 176
    studio system antitrust case, 70
    See also Citizens United v. Federal Election Commission

U.S. Treasury Department, 112–113

Uygur, Cenk, 39

Vermont, 93

Vietnam War, 76, 140, 187

voting rights, 177, 187–188

"wage inflation," 35, 156, 166

wages, fair, 160–163, 165, 167, 200

Wahhabi Movement, 125–126

Wall Street, 100, 114–118, 166, 183–184

war, 117, 125, 146–150, 200. *See also* military

Washington, George, 1–2, 24, 31

wealthy
    benefits of taxing the, 10–11, 37, 43, 136–137
    and the credit trap, 166–167
    "free trade" boon to, 157–159
    Great Tax Con, 38–43, 48–50
    "investor class," 166, 201
    ownership of media by, 38–39, 41
    Rite of the First Night, 191–192, 194, 196
    Swiss bank accounts of, 101
    tax cuts and the, 33–38, 195–196
    working class serving the, 197
    See also corporate oligarchy

Welch, Jack, 155–156, 158, 159

WellPoint's Anthem Blue Cross, 184

Wilson, Woodrow, 49

Winship, Michael, 185

Wisconsin, 107–108

Woodley Herber, 98

worker-owned cooperatives, 14, 192–194, 196–197

working class
    conservatives' views of, 171–172
    dependency on credit, 166–167
    fair wages and illegal immigration, 161–163
    historic labor struggle, 160–161
    outsourcing and the, 155–160
    role of, 197
    taxing the wealthy to benefit, 33–36, 43, 48–49
    Teddy Roosevelt's fight for, 200
    See also middle class

World Trade Organization (WTO), 25, 29, 157

Wyden, Ron, 93, 94

About the Author

Thom Hartmann is the four-time Project Censored Award–winning, best-selling author of more than 20 books in print in 15 languages on five continents and the number one progressive radio and TV talk-show host in the United States, also carried on radio stations in Europe and Africa, syndicated by Pacifica, Dial-Global, and Free Speech TV.

His work has inspired several movies, including one produced and narrated by Leonardo DiCaprio. He has met in personal audiences with, at the invitation of, both Pope John Paul II and the Dalai Lama. He's built several successful businesses and for more than 20 years did international relief work in almost a dozen countries for the international Salem organization based in Germany.

Thom and his wife, Louise, founded a community for abused children and a school for learning-disabled children in New Hampshire, and he has helped launch famine relief, agricultural development, leprosy treatment, orphan care, and hospital programs in Uganda, Colombia, India, and Russia.

Also by Thom Hartmann from Berrett-Koehler Publishers

Unequal Protection
How Corporations Became "People"—and How You Can Fight Back

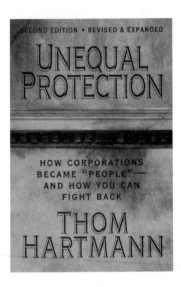

Unequal Protection tells the astonishing story of how, after decades of sensible limits on corporate power, an offhand, off-the-record comment by a Supreme Court justice in the mid-nineteenth century led to the Fourteenth Amendment—intended to grant basic rights to freed slaves—becoming the justification for granting corporations the same rights as human beings. Thom outlines the destructive consequences and proposes specific legal remedies that will finally put an end to the bizarre farce of corporate personhood. This thoroughly updated edition features his analysis of recent landmark Supreme Court cases, including *Citizens United v. Federal Election Commission*, which tossed out corporate campaign finance limits.

Paperback, 384 pages, ISBN 978-1-60509-559-2
PDF ebook, ISBN 978-1-60509-560-8

Berrett–Koehler Publishers, Inc.
www.bkconnection.com

800.929.2929

Cracking the Code
How to Win Hearts, Change Minds, and Restore America's Original Vision

How can we connect with the millions of Americans who have bought into the right-wing line? Drawing on his background as a psychotherapist, advertising executive, and radio host, Thom applies what science has learned about how people actually perceive information to give you the tools you need to make the progressive message even more compelling and persuasive.

Hardcover, 240 pages, ISBN 978-1-57675-458-0
Paperback, ISBN 978-1-57675-627-0
PDF ebook, ISBN 978-1-57675-533-4

Screwed
The Undeclared War Against the Middle Class—and What We Can Do About It

Starting with Ronald Reagan and accelerating under George W. Bush, American policy makers have waged an assault on the middle class, the very foundation of American democracy, as seen by the Founding Fathers. Thom chronicles this assault and recommends actions people can take to restore a prosperous middle class and keep America strong.

Paperback, 264 pages, ISBN 978-1-57675-463-4
PDF ebook, ISBN 978-1-57675-529-7

BK Berrett–Koehler Publishers, Inc.
www.bkconnection.com   800.929.2929

Berrett–Koehler
Publishers

Berrett-Koehler is an independent publisher dedicated to an ambitious mission: *Creating a World That Works for All*.

We believe that to truly create a better world, action is needed at all levels— individual, organizational, and societal. At the individual level, our publications help people align their lives with their values and with their aspirations for a better world. At the organizational level, our publications promote progressive leadership and management practices, socially responsible approaches to business, and humane and effective organizations. At the societal level, our publications advance social and economic justice, shared prosperity, sustainability, and new solutions to national and global issues.

A major theme of our publications is "Opening Up New Space." Berrett-Koehler titles challenge conventional thinking, introduce new ideas, and foster positive change. Their common quest is changing the underlying beliefs, mindsets, institutions, and structures that keep generating the same cycles of problems, no matter who our leaders are or what improvement programs we adopt.

We strive to practice what we preach—to operate our publishing company in line with the ideas in our books. At the core of our approach is stewardship, which we define as a deep sense of responsibility to administer the company for the benefit of all of our "stakeholder" groups: authors, customers, employees, investors, service providers, and the communities and environment around us.

We are grateful to the thousands of readers, authors, and other friends of the company who consider themselves to be part of the "BK Community." We hope that you, too, will join us in our mission.

A BK Currents Book

This book is part of our BK Currents series. BK Currents books advance social and economic justice by exploring the critical intersections between business and society. Offering a unique combination of thoughtful analysis and progressive alternatives, BK Currents books promote positive change at the national and global levels. To find out more, visit **www.bkconnection.com**.

Berrett–Koehler Publishers

A community dedicated to creating
a world that works for all

Visit Our Website: www.bkconnection.com

Read book excerpts, see author videos and Internet movies, read our authors' blogs, join discussion groups, download book apps, find out about the BK Affiliate Network, browse subject-area libraries of books, get special discounts, and more!

Subscribe to Our Free E-Newsletter, the *BK Communiqué*

Be the first to hear about new publications, special discount offers, exclusive articles, news about bestsellers, and more! Get on the list for our free e-newsletter by going to **www.bkconnection.com**.

Get Quantity Discounts

Berrett-Koehler books are available at quantity discounts for orders of ten or more copies. Please call us toll-free at (800) 929-2929 or email us at **bkp .orders@aidcvt.com**.

Join the BK Community

BKcommunity.com is a virtual meeting place where people from around the world can engage with kindred spirits to create a world that works for all. BKcommunity.com members may create their own profiles, blog, start and participate in forums and discussion groups, post photos and videos, answer surveys, announce and register for upcoming events, and chat with others online in real time. Please join the conversation!